Thank God For RAW
Recipes for Health

Written by:

Julie Wandling

Published by: Hallelujah Acres Publishing
                 900 South Post Road
                 Shelby, NC 28150

Distributed by: Hallelujah Acres Publishing
                 P.O. Box 2388
                 900 South Post Road
                 Shelby, NC 28150
                 (704) 481-1700
                 www.hacres.com

Text copyright 2002 by Julie Wandling

The contents of this book are a reflection of the author's experience and are in no way intended to take the place of professional medical treatment. The author does not give medical advice or prescribe any technique as a form of treatment for physical, mental or emotional health challenges with or without the advice of a physician.

This book is dedicated to
God and Mom.

Acknowledgements

I need to say a special "thank you" to Judy who conducted the interviews for this book. She is a wonderful friend. And to my mom, Gloria, who has mentored me through this whole process with encouragement and love. A big thanks to Gramps, who happily eats all my mistakes and leftovers! Thank you to my husband, Bob, who has graciously put up with me these last several years, through my pains, illnesses and struggles. To Diana, whose story is so encouraging, and Becky, whose story will stir your heart. To my boys, Corbin and Ryan, who eat bananas when they would rather have candy! To Lisa, who sets a good example of a great mom. Thank you to Scott for his guidance and encouragement. Thanks to Rev. Malkmus for his courage in sharing the message, "You don't have to be sick!"

Julie Wandling
rwandling@neo.rr.com

Thank God For Raw
Table of Contents

Recipes for Health

Introduction

Are you sick and tired of being sick and tired? Are you afraid of cancer? Overweight? Fatigued? In pain? I was all of these things and many more just 15 months ago! Now, after finding the truth about nutrition, I can happily say none of the above describe me anymore. I thank God every day for showing me the way to health, and putting people in my life at just the right times to help me learn. I pray this book and the ones I suggest will help you find your way.

Foreword

Just when you think you've read it all someone comes along and puts an entirely new slant on things. This book is one of those. A fresh pair of eyes, an enthusiastic mindset, positive life experiences and creative energy have combined in an offering that is fresh and delightful. This book is not the final word on diet reform, nor does it pretend to be. It does not proport to offer cures for every condition under the sun. It does not give endless case histories, or make unsubstantiated health claims. What it does, however, it does very well. It tells one person's story, and gives one person's perspective. It is a moving and inspiring story, with a motivating outcome. It is a story well worth telling and repeating, as it will have a positive effect on anyone who hears or reads it. Lives will be saved.

SuperMan could jump to the top of the Empire State Building in a single bound. The rest of us take the stairs. This book uses the staircase, for sure, and that is its strength. Everyone knows that successful dietary and lifestyle reforms require time. Few put a plan into action. Most people take so many detours (due to the influences of market forces, fads, and misinformation) disguised as health guidance that they never ever get even close to truly living healthfully. Within these pages many of the necessary steps to achieving a healthier lifestyle are defined. It is an onward and upward process.

Enjoy your read, have fun on your health journey, and know that the view from the top will be as good for you as it is for anyone, no matter what speed you take. Healthful living is well worth the effort.

Dr. Douglas N. Graham,
author of "Grain Damage", "Nutrition and Athletic Performance", "The High Energy Diet Recipe Guide", "Perpetual Health", and "Hygienic Fasting".
www.doctorgraham.cc

Chapter 1

My Story

Recipes for Health

Thank God For RAW ▼

My Story

Almost two years ago, I weighed 315 pounds and had blood pressure of 199/100. One day in January, 2000, I swore I had a heart attack! I had serious pain across my chest and back. The next day I went to our family doctor who dismissed me saying, "You're too young to have a heart attack." I was 35 and weighed over 300 pounds. Hello! On February 23, 2000, the doctor told me I had to immediately begin taking blood pressure medication "for the rest of my life." I looked in the mirror and saw my huge gut sticking out and knew the reason for this crisis. I left her office, prescription in hand, and decided to immediately change my lifestyle instead. The idea sounded good, but I didn't have a clue! In the past, I had tried all the fad diets, including vegetarian, which obviously failed me. So what to do?

About two years ago, my health-seeking mom came across this diet of raw foods. She happily announced one day that she no longer had to cook her food. It sounded silly to me so I ignored her. I was the Betty Crocker of Northeast Ohio, for crying out loud! Not cook my food? How do you have cheesecake without cooking it? Well, after that doctor's appointment, I decided to give Mom's whacky new diet a try. Mind you, Mom was 60-something and bouncing around all the time while I was hauling my huge back side up a flight of stairs. I was even afraid to sit in peoples' chairs! Talk about embarrassing.

I had heard enough preaching from Mom to get started so I didn't tell anyone what I was doing. I just did it. No pressure from the outside. You should have seen my family when I started throwing all their favorite foods into a bag for the church's food pantry! Gone were the Fruit Loops, milk, chicken wings, potato chips, Oreos, ice cream, hot dogs, etc. My family thought I was insane!

Then, after about two weeks of eating salad, I called Mom for ideas. She was thrilled I was finally listening to her for once in my life! She gave me a bunch of books to read so I could understand the whole process better. There is no fear in knowledge. I had the best time reading about nutrition this past year. I have probably read 200 books. Much of what I read, I already knew from my past dieting attempts; the rest was fascinating.

After putting into action the plan in the next chapter, my life turned around. Within five weeks, my blood pressure was 156/96, without medication. It is now 120/70! My energy was abounding. My friends were scared, I was bouncing off the walls at times! I have, to date, lost 100 pounds! I feel wonderful! People say "I glow." My hair grows beautifully, my skin is always soft and holds a tan longer. My feet, back and knees don't ache constantly anymore. I made it through the entire winter without a cold for the first time ever!

The key for me was the realization that God didn't make me the sick, fat lady. I did. Boy, did that give me HOPE!

Chapter 2
The Knowledge & The Plan

Recipes for Health

I came to the conclusion that I made myself a sick, fat lady after reading *Why Christians Get Sick* by Rev. George Malkmus. He says that God provided us with the perfect diet in Genesis 1:29 — a diet of fruits, vegetables, nuts and seeds. Rev. Malkmus also suggests that the first people on Earth ate their foods raw, which makes sense to me. I can't picture Eve, in the buff, baking apple pies. He outlines three reasons why we get sick: to glorify God, as a result of sin, and as a result of our diets, the third being the reason for most of us.

His book, *God's Way to Ultimate Health*, helped me understand more about how my body works, especially my colon. I don't think mine was working very well because right after I started eating all those salads, I had some unbelievable "bathroom moments!" Rev. Malkmus recommends eating a diet consisting of 75-85% raw foods with the balance being cooked vegetables and or grains.

Rev. Malkmus's wife, Rhonda, wrote a book titled *Recipes for Life from God's Garden*. Her recipes are lots of fun to play around with. In it she tells of the "five-whites" we should avoid:

1 white fat (meat)
2 white milk (cow's)
3 white flour
4 white sugar and
5 white salt

An amazing concept came to me from Rev. Malkmus: *a self-healing body*. Wow. He suggests God gave us all a self-healing body. We are fearfully and wonderfully made. We just need to give it the proper nourishment and it will work just fine. Cool. I am not so sure I'll never be sick again, but I sure do look and feel a whole lot better!

Harvey Diamond has some excellent books, *Fit For Life I*, and *II* and *A New Beginning*. He lays out a plan for healthy eating which has helped me. I needed a plan. He suggests eating fruit in the morning when your body is trying to eliminate yesterday's fare so you don't stop the process by redirecting your energy to digestion. Then take in most of your foods during the day, stopping in the early evening. He also recommends mostly raw foods. His third book, *Fit for Life: A New Beginning*, gives fascinating information about our lymph systems. I was amazed to find out that the tonsils are part of the lymph system trying to clean out our heads. No wonder they get inflamed.

I also like his idea of "mono-dieting" to give the body a break from hard digestive work. He suggests eating lightly of one kind of food for a day or so. One of his mono-diets is what is known as "juice fasting." I have done this four times so far for three and four

days at a time. After the first time, I knew one thing... I eat way too much food! I didn't keel over or starve to death! In fact, it feels wonderful. When you do this, your body begins detoxifying itself by eliminating toxins. Before detoxification can be done efficiently, the colon must be relatively cleaned out. This can be accomplished by eating fruits and veggies for several months. The fiber from them works like a broom sweeping away the debris. So, I waited for about three months to try it. The first night, I dreamed of pizza, even though I hadn't had it for three months! When my dreams went from pizza to nectarines, I knew I was doing the right thing!

Another great source of information has been a number of videos by Dr. Lorraine Day. She tells it like it is, buddy! Her 10-step plan helped her to become cancer-free after having breast cancer. Her 10 steps are these:

1. Nutrition through raw foods
2. Rest
3. Pure water: 8-10 glasses a day
4. Daily exercise
5. Sunshine on the body everyday
6. Fresh air
7. Moderation (opposite of gluttony)
8. Benevolence, doing things for others
9. An Attitude of gratitude
10. Trust in God

Her video *He Loves Me, He Loves Me Not* is totally inspirational. I like to use her video titled, *You Can't Improve On God.* That is so true.

John Robbins gives some scary information about our meat and dairy these days in *Diet for a New America*. It's out in book and video. I watched the video with my kids. That was a turning point for them. They were saddened by the conditions in which the animals were kept. Ryan cried when he watched the baby chicks getting de-beaked. My boys now understand that a hamburger is really a cow's behind! His new book, *The Food Revolution*, amazes and sickens me. Everyone on the planet needs to read this book. The boys and I read sections every day. We are slowly, but surely, destroying our own futures through our demand for meat.

Where do you get your protein and calcium? I get asked that question every day! The same place I get every other nutrient I need: fresh fruits, vegetables, nuts and seeds. Look at any nutrition chart in any book and you will see that fruits and veggies are loaded with vitamins and minerals. In fact, in the news we are constantly hearing recommendations to eat more fruit and vegetables, and less red meat. Soy and rice milks are fortified with calcium and vitamin D. Exposure to sunlight helps the body make its own vitamin D. Another good reason to get outdoors in the fresh air!

A second great source for meat education is Howard Lyman, The Mad Cowboy. On his website, he talks about the animal feed used today, the hormones and antibiotics. Our cows are not eating grass anymore. They are kept from being vegetarian, their natural, created state.

Both Rev. Malkmus and Dr. Day recommend juicing everyday, especially carrots. I try to juice organic produce as much as possible to avoid loads of poisons in our juice. The Juiceman's *Power of Juicing* is a great book for ideas on juicing. He gives nutritional info and wonderful recipes. I like the way he explains the benefits of juice, too. I started drinking mustard greens in my carrot juice for muscle cramps and they really helped. We did have to learn the hard way that they are really HOT! I told Mom to try them but forgot to tell her the hot part. She juiced the whole bunch and burned her throat. Green juices are a big source of calcium so I hide them in our carrot juice, which is really sweet. I also save our scraps from fruits and veggies to juice, like lettuce cores, celery bottoms and tops, broccoli stems, cantaloupe skin, goop and seeds, pineapple cores, etc. I read once that our trash cans eat better than we do! Strain your juice in a little metal strainer right over your glass, stirring it with a spoon to press it through. You will get less fiber, helping the juice to digest faster—in about 20 minutes. Then wait awhile to eat so as not to mix the juice with foods that take longer to exit the stomach.

Unfortunately, these books and hundreds of others are not readily available through local bookstores or libraries. So, Mom and I have started our own health consulting ministry under the name Healthy for Him. We have been able to help people buy books, juicers and supplements such as BarleyMax and Fiber Cleanse. BarleyMax is one of the most nutrient-dense foods you can eat, made from the juice of young barley plants. Fiber Cleanse is a natural bulking food that helps cleanse the colon. I enjoy helping people put together their own plan.

Two classy ladies taught me about the spiritual aspects of the raw foods diet. Jannie Wilcoxson and Catherine Williams. They are Bible teachers who've got it going on. I learned from them that my body is not my own. Jannie says, "How can we Christians tell a dying world about a living Saviour, if we are always sick and tired?" Amen!

My mentor for both the raw diet and exercise has been Dr. Doug Graham. He is wonderfully available over the internet at www.vegsource.com <http://www.vegsource. com> on the Raw Foods and Sports Nutrition board. His book *Nutrition and Athletic Performance* is a must read for everyone, athlete or not. We call it the banana book! I make his sports drinks for my boys and they love them. Gramps likes the Banana Milk Sports Drink after his runs. Bye-bye Gatorade! Another book of his, *Grain Damage*, blew my mind. Who knew I was sluggish from wheat? Opioids in my bread. Geez. The chemicals used in processing bread don't need to be in me. So, we are eating our whole grain, organic breads in moderation these days. The good doc says that if you're still craving breadstuffs and pastas, you're not eating enough fruit.

Remember Hosea 4:6, My people perish from lack of knowledge.

Chapter 3
The Food

Recipes for Health

After reading all these books and feeling better by the day, I had to figure out how to eat mostly raw foods without getting really bored and spending the family fortune. I worked in catering for a few years but had no idea what to do with fruits and vegetables in their natural form. The boys and I took a field trip to the grocery store and asked the produce manager to give us a tour, which he was happy to do. We asked lots of questions about taste and preparation methods of everything on the shelves. He confirmed that organic produce is far better for you than commercially grown due to the use of pesticides, fertilizers and waxes. It won't always look as pretty but it will taste much sweeter. Also, keep your eyes open for labels saying "*No GMO's*" (Genetically Modified Organisms). In my opinion, we do not have proof that these "foods" are safe or healthy. Only time will tell.

So what do we eat?

I start with fruit since we are supposed to eat our fruit first to help our bodies clean out.

APPLES, every day. Juice apples with carrots and eat apples out of hand. Last fall, we tried about every apple available. It was fun experimenting with all the different varieties. Some were mushy, some tart, but all were very good. We still don't know which are which but we know we like apples! We always buy organic apples, as they are not waxed or grown using pesticides. My favorites are Braeburn, Fuji, Gala, and Pink Ladies.

ORANGES—boy, do we love oranges! My grandpa lives in Florida and grows oranges and tangerines. He sent us a huge box in January. Ryan ate eight tangerines the day it arrived! I have been buying them ever since. The clementines were awesome this year. We had never had them before. They are very easy to peel; the boys can do it themselves. A big plus. Mineolas are great on a spinach salad with poppy seed dressing. Oranges last quite awhile in the fruit basket so I don't refrigerate them. Oranges are better in season - they tend to be tough otherwise.

GRAPES, great for the sweet tooth. I like to buy 3-4 different colors and mix them up in a huge bowl. This makes a nice party snack. I often pack a container of grapes to take with us on the road. Organic grapes are much sweeter than commercially grown ones so I try to find them whenever possible. The only time I found grapes to be too expensive was in the dead of winter. If I am feeling a sugar rush from my grapes, I just eat some celery to slow it down. Frozen seedless grapes make a nice summertime treat for the kids, too.

PEARS, mmm, I love pears. Corbin eats pears every day. They are good all year round. I like the red ones and the boys like the D'Anjou ones. Asian pears are crunchier and good on salads. Pears run through the juicer will give you pearsauce, like applesauce. Pears are

best when stored out of the fridge until they are fully ripe. If you have any left, then put them in the fridge for a day or two.

BANANAS, you can do a million things with bananas. Best of all is to just "peel and eat!" Sometimes, when we are really hungry or in a hurry, we will just down two to three bananas each. Talk about fast food! My mom puts bananas in her salad dressings to make them creamy. Frozen bananas make awesome ice cream when run through a Champion juicer. A blender will give you wonderful shakes or smoothies. Peel your bananas and freeze them in a big freezer bag or just freeze them in the peel then run them under hot water until the skins pop off. My freezer is full of them all the time. Many people think pesticides and fertilizers don't penetrate the banana peel, but I am here to tell you they do! Organic bananas are much smaller and much sweeter than commercially grown ones. I leave the bananas out until the last one turns brown, then he joins the stash in the freezer.

PEACHES AND NECTARINES, Corbin's favorites. I only buy them when in season, however. The ones that come in early from Chile are hard and lacking in flavor. Patience definitely pays off when you eat that first peach of the season. Here's a cool science experiment: Rinse off your peach pits and let them dry in a sunny window. Take them to the sidewalk and rub them for hours and days on the concrete until they are smooth like a stone. My boys had several "stones" in the making in their pockets last summer. Just make sure they take them out before you do the wash! This is a great reason for them to eat their peaches.

MELONS, another favorite in our house. Cantaloupe, musk melon (honeydew) and watermelons. I can't wait until watermelon is in season again. This is another one worth waiting for. Cantaloupes and honeydews are good most of the year round. They get more expensive in the winter, but when you don't buy meat, you can afford more expensive melons. I buy melons, wash them on the outside, and cut them into chunks. I store them in plastic containers in the fridge. The outsides, seeds and goop can be juiced.

PINEAPPLES, Mom brought home fresh-picked pineapples from Hawaii a few months ago. They were sooo good. I always buy the most expensive pineapples here, however. The big yellow ones. Try one, you will be amazed at the difference. And $5.00 is a pretty cheap meal for three! The grocer may have a pineapple corer on location to core it for you. If not, cut off the top, then down the sides. Cut around the core and save it to juice with some kale. Cut the strips into chunks and store them in plastic containers, if you don't eat the whole thing like we do. Corbin likes to roll his chunks in dried, unsulphured, unsweetened coconut.

KIWIS, Ryan's favorite. He cuts them in half and scoops them out with a spoon. Gramps eats his skin and all.

LEMONS, the cure for Coke-aholics. I juiced a whole lemon in 16 ounces of water every day for the first three months to get over my Coca-Cola addiction. It gives you that afterbite you get from soda pop. If you need to, you can add a teaspoon of honey.

DRIED FRUITS, dates, figs, prunes and raisins are our favorites. Make sure to buy organic, unsulphured and unsweetened dried fruits. When they are dried, you get a more concentrated poisoning from commercially grown fruits.

STRAWBERRIES, I can't wait until June! Last year, we picked enough strawberries to fill a fourth of the freezer for smoothies in the winter. Definitely make sure to buy organic strawberries. The pesticides and fertilizers are stored in the seeds on the outsides of this fruit.

BLACKBERRIES, BLUEBERRIES AND RASPBERRIES, These are best when purchased in season. You can buy boatloads of them in June and July. Eat as many as you can, then freeze the rest for smoothies and pancakes.

As you can see, I left out tons of fruits. I recommend you experiment to find what kinds you like. Learning to love fruit has been both fun and tasty! Anything with seeds still in it is classified as a fruit.

Next comes veggies, the builders. Fresh, raw vegetables are loaded with vitamins, minerals, enzymes and antioxidants.

CARROTS, juiced everyday with apples and greens. Baby carrots are great for snacks with almond butter or dressing. Babies can use baby carrots right out of the fridge to teeth on.

SALAD GREENS, romaine, red and green lettuces, radicchio, endive, escarole, bibb lettuce, spinach, dandelion greens, chard, baby greens, etc. I usually buy two or three of these at a time. Wash them well in ¼ cup vinegar to a sinkful of cool water. Rinse them and lay them out on dishtowels to dry or use a salad spinner. Break them up by hand and mix them. Put them in a large bowl with a paper towel in the bottom to soak up water. I usually buy five pounds of greens a week for my family of four.

RED BELL PEPPERS, couldn't live without them. (I learned recently that green peppers are not ripe which is why they make you burp.) I eat red bell peppers every day on my

salads. Great source of vitamin C. I do not cut them up to store. The cut edges will get slimy. So, I just cut off what I need and put the whole pepper back in a storage bag in the fridge. Watch out for waxed peppers.

RED ONIONS, also great on salad. These are my salad onion of choice. I use other onions in salad dressings at times and green onions on Asian salads.

BROCCOLI—calcium, you say? I make the kids eat raw broccoli every day since they no longer get calcium from animals. They have learned to like it. We eat the florets and juice the stalks. Broccoli is also 49% protein. Go figure. And broccoli is always cheap.

CAULIFLOWER, sometimes expensive but worth it. Cauliflower holds up nicely in prepared salads. Keep some cut up in a bowl with broccoli, carrots and snow peas for easy dipping.

CELERY, the best source of natural sodium. It is good in juices, salads and for dipping.

CUCUMBERS—refreshing! I love cucumbers in my carrot juice. They make a great salad dressing base in the blender. I always have cucumber in our salads. Make sure you are buying organic cukes. If you can't find organic, peel them. The wax will never come off by washing.

GARLIC, eat some every day for good health and bad breath. Funny, but true. Buy whole bulbs of garlic. Pop out the cloves one at a time when you need one. Peel and chop it or squash it in a garlic press. Fresh garlic is awesome in salad dressings.

GINGERROOT, tricky but yummy. The first time I bought fresh ginger, I thought it was rotten. It smells like Lemon Pledge! A ginger grater works best, but if you don't have one use the old metal grater on the small-hole side. You do have to peel it. This is great for salad dressings of the Asian variety.

BRUSSEL SPROUTS, crunchy raw. I like to peel off the outer layer and discard. Then I keep peeling and use those leaves in my salads. The boys like theirs lightly steamed but still crunchy.

AVOCADOS, I love avocados now. I always thought I couldn't eat them because they were high in fat. It turns out they are high in the fats we actually need, not at all like animal fats. Cut around the avocado lengthwise then break in half. Pop out the pit then scoop out the flesh. It makes a great creamy dip and salad dressing base. Or, try cutting them up on a salad.

NUTS—almonds, couldn't live without them! I eat raw almonds every day either by the handful or as almond butter. The Champion juicer makes wonderful raw nut butters. Raw nuts are great for the proteins we need. After hard exercise, I find almond butter and carrots to be very satisfying. There are several other nuts you can eat raw such as pecans, walnuts, pine nuts, cashews, filberts, Brazil nuts. In the fall, we ate pounds of in-shell mixed nuts. I have read that if you have trouble digesting nuts that you can soak them for a few hours to break down the enzyme inhibitor, which stops them from growing in the cupboard.

SEEDS, sunflower, pumpkin, sesame and flax are the most popular among raw foodists. I love seeds on my salad. Raw pumpkin seeds are sometimes called "pepitos" and are green. Try to buy unhulled sesame seeds for the most calcium, they have more calcium than milk. Flax seeds are the best source for omega-3 fatty acids. Grind them first in a coffee grinder to release the oils and aid digestion. Top your salads with them daily. They can also be added to smoothies to give them extra thickness. Mix them with water, equal parts, for a slimy egg replacer, which can be used as a binder in baking. All seeds are great in granolas as are nuts.

SPROUTS, great on salads or even juiced if you grow too many to eat right away. Sprouting is ridiculously easy. Just wash out a quart-sized canning jar, save the ring part of the lid or buy sprouting lids at the store. Put in a few tablespoons of seeds and cover them with water. Let them soak for 4-6 hours then rinse them off. Leave the jar upside down to drain. Rinse and drain them several times a day until the sprouts are to the desired length. Start them in the sink then move them to a sunny window once the seed starts to sprout to promote the production of chlorophyll - usually 3-5 days. Rinse them one last time then store in the fridge. Rinse again before eating. Common sprouting seeds are alfalfa, radish, clover, mung bean, lentil, and broccoli.

BREADS, aah, the smell of freshly baked bread! I think it is best to bake your own breads from whole grains, but we can't all do that. So, the next best thing would be to buy locally baked breads that contain no white flour, sugar or preservatives. Sprouted breads from *Food for Life* are also very good. Some raw recipe books have recipes for sprouted dehydrated breads. I have tried several but don't care for them, so I have left them out of the recipe section. Grains are very mucus forming and slightly acidic and should be used only in moderation.

FATS/OILS, extra virgin, cold pressed olive oil, flax oil, hemp oil or Udo's oil should be our oils of choice. These oils supply essential fatty acids. However, these fats will also be

found in nuts, seeds, avocados and many other vegetables. So, we don't have to rely on these oils for the necessary fats. Any of these oils can be used in any of the recipes in this book. Many people suggest eating one tablespoon of flax oil a day for a year to rebuild your supply of essential fatty acids. Buy the freshest oils possible, check the dates, and use them quickly. Oils go rancid very fast, especially flax. If it smells "off," don't eat it. If you need oil for cooking, use only olive oil. The others should not be heated.

HERBS, I like herbs for seasonings in salads and dressings. You will see several recipes including herbs in the back. I also enjoy herbal teas in the evening. Again, buy organic whenever possible.

So, what cooked stuff do we eat?

Well, we like baked potatoes (especially sweet potatoes!), green beans, corn-on-the cob, brown rice, whole grain breads, whole-grain pastas, and some soy "meats," and vegetable stir fry. But these things come after our dinner salads or cut veggies on most days.

Chapter 4
The Family

Recipes for Health

My two boys, Corbin and Ryan, are perfect angels who eat whatever I give them and do exactly as they are told. Yeah, right!

DISCIPLINE, EDUCATION AND PATIENCE: the keys to successfully changing your kids' diets. Explain to them why they must drink carrot juice, then make them drink it! It has taken them some time to come around but they are adjusting. One thing is certain: they are getting plenty of nutrition. Corbin grew four inches last year and Ryan, two–and–a–half. These are their basic rules: First, drink your juice. Wait a half hour, then eat some fruit. If they are still hungry, they can have some granola or sometimes I will make a hot cereal or pancakes. It is usually lunchtime by then. During the day, they have more fruit and trail mixes. They also enjoy nut butter and jelly sandwiches. Dinner always starts with salad or cut veggies.

Their favorite brand name meat replacers are BOCA nuggets, BOCA burgers, BOCA sausages, Gardenburgers, YVES tofu dogs, Fantastic Brand taco mix and chili mix. These are in no way ideal, so fruits and veggies always come first—always fresh and raw!

Getting my kids involved in the food selection has also helped. I give each of them a dollar and let them buy whatever they want from the produce section of the grocery. Ryan always buys something cute and little, just like him, usually kiwis, apricots, berries or kumquats. They love to play around with dates, coconut, figs, nuts, seeds and raisins. It is amazing what can you do with these simple ingredients. There are several recipes they have made up in the recipe section. And how easy is it to tell them to get the cut veggies out of the fridge for lunch. They can pack their own foods for the days we are out. I home school my sons; if they went to school, they could easily pack their own lunches the same way. Bananas, apples, trail mix and a bottle of water. No need for refrigeration or reheating. Who said you can only eat one piece at a time? We have been known to eat several apples and a couple of bananas in one sitting. If God expected us to eat just one banana, why did he put them in bunches!

I rarely, if ever, allow soda pop, chocolate, cookies, candies, bottled juices, etc., at home. Even at parties I try to discourage it but I can't always be there. With a little education and experience, they, too, will realize what these things really are and what happens when they eat them. Ryan came home one Wednesday night after church saying his tummy hurt and he was shaky. He had eaten cupcakes and candy all night. Corbin was coming home from Sunday morning church very, very sleepy and never hungry. I finally asked him if he had been eating at church. He said, "Yes, my teacher lets me earn doughnuts for saying my verse and bringing my Bible and I have doughnuts in Junior Worship." "Hmmm, don't feel that way after eating bananas do ya, son?".

Thank God For RAW

Both boys have seen great improvements in their health. Prior to changing eating habits, one had bad ear infections and the other a nasty rash and big-time mucus. All are gone and only return when they have several "junk-food days" in a row. They are learning.

Chapter 5
The Exercise

Recipes for Health

Oh, how I used to despise that word! I thought that in order to exercise, I had to do aerobics, so I didn't exercise at all. All that sweating, bouncing, jumping. Ugh! I counted chasing kids and keeping house as my exercise. Each time I went up and down the steps with laundry, I figured I had exercised. Not!

One of the coolest things about this raw foods diet is the increased energy. Nowadays, you couldn't stop me from exercising. One day, I woke up and just had to move. I started by walking around the house then around the block. Now, I can easily go four miles. I started getting books from the library on different kinds of exercises as my energy kept increasing. Mixing up my routines has helped me stay interested and find muscles I forgot all about.

If you are a beginner exerciser, as I was not long ago, look for beginners' books. Then just *do what YOU can do*, not necessarily what the pretty lady in spandex in the picture can do! For beginners, I suggest stretching exercises. You will be amazed at how tight your body is and how limber it can become. Stretching has loosened up my poor old back immensely. I was living on muscle relaxers for two years because my back couldn't support my weight. Yes, losing the weight helps, but it's not the whole picture. To strengthen your back, you have to strengthen your stomach. You know that bulge? It can be sucked back in with a little effort. I'm still working on mine and can't wait until it's gone!

Weights are also very helpful for toning and strength. I started with two-pound weights a few months ago and am now at 10 pounds. I have these cool little muscles growing on my arms and shoulders. My underarm flab is going away nicely.

Swimming is a great exercise for those of us who don't like sweat! You can sweat and not even realize it. I started eight months ago swimming once a week during my kids' swimming lessons. At first, I went four to five laps (laps being one trip down the lane…72 one-time trips is a mile.) I am up to 50 now! It takes me an hour, and I have to rest sometimes, but I keep on keeping on. I mix up the strokes, too. I wish I could talk more of the moms into joining me. We have to be there with the kids anyway.

I picked up some books on water aerobics and took the jumping exercises from them. Any exercise that makes your flab change directions will firm it up. So, I find jumping and twisting exercises to do in the water to tone the muscles but not hurt my knees.

Deep breathing exercises have been very helpful. I no longer get winded walking up steps or exercising. It has even helped my singing in the choir by giving me the lung capacity to hold notes longer. These exercises are so easy. I use tapes by Greer Childers.

Thank God For RAW ▼

My pal, Tamra, talked me into hiking our local Metroparks Trails last fall with my boys. I was afraid of the high places but really enjoyed myself. The boys loved it and are ready to go again. There is something to be said for exercising outdoors in the fresh air, makes me feel alive!

My mom does rebounding. She has a little mini-trampoline and jumps on it every day. She says it doesn't hurt the knees and is great for getting the lymph system to move out those toxins. Also, your flab changes directions so this would help tone it up. Mom is "60-something." If she can do this, so can you!

Look for opportunities to exercise. In my life, I have found time to exercise while my kids are taking lessons. I even exercise at the church in the gym while they are playing. During their choir practice, I go to a quiet room and stretch. If I weren't doing this, I know I would just be sitting, talking and eating. Fellowship is nice, so I try to encourage my pals to exercise with me and talk then.

The bottom line is this: *Start eating right, gain energy, and get moving!*

Chapter 6
The Tips

Recipes for Health

TIPS FOR SHOPPING

Seek out a store with organic produce. Even if you have to go out of your way, work it into your routine. Buy as much organic produce as possible. If what you want is too pricey, choose to make something else!

<u>My average weekly shopping for my family of 4:</u>

4-5 pounds of salad greens
6-10 pounds oranges when in season
5 pounds bananas
25 pounds carrots for juicing
6 pounds apples for eating and juicing
1 cabbage
3 pounds red onions
3 avocados
3-5 pounds pears
1 cantaloupe
1 pineapple
6 kiwis
5 pounds potatoes
2 bunches of greens for juicing: kale, collards, dandelion, turnip
2 red bell peppers
2 cucumbers
1 zucchini
1-2 broccoli
1 cauliflower
2 bags baby carrots
5 pounds grapes
1 box vegetable burgers
1 pack soy hot dogs
1 box whole grain pasta
pasta sauce
1 gallon soy milk
2 loaves of whole grain bakery bread
extra fruits when in season
5-10 gallons of distilled water

Thank God For RAW

Monthly Bulk Shopping:

These things should be available at your local health food stores.
1 bottle shoyu or tamari (not raw)
32 ounces pure maple syrup (not raw)
16 ounces raw honey
5 pounds raw almonds
5 pounds sunflower seeds
2 pounds pumpkin seeds
5-10 pounds oats
32 ounces extra virgin, cold pressed olive oil
16 ounces flax oil
1 pound flax seeds
1 pound sesame seeds
3 pounds dates
3 pounds figs
3 pounds prunes
1 pound pecans
1 pound walnuts
seasonings and herbs
2 pounds brown rice
16 oz sea salt
sprouting seeds
2 pounds whole-grain pancake mix

TIPS FOR "AWAY-FROM-HOME" DAYS

1. Get an insulated food bag or cooler.
2. Get a spill-proof water bottle for each person. Carry it with you everywhere!
3. Juice ahead up to three days and store in the fridge or cooler in canning jars to carry with you.
4. Pack foods that don't squish! Apples, bowls of grapes, peeled oranges, bags of cut veggies and almond butter, etc. Carrying food with you at all times will make stopping at fast-food places unnecessary.
5. Keep trail mixes, nuts or granolas in the car for emergency purposes. A gallon of distilled water stores nicely in the trunk to refill your bottles.

TIPS FOR EATING OUT

1. Don't! Invite everyone to your house!
2. Call the restaurant to see if they have at least romaine lettuce.
3. Order your salad with all the raw vegetables they have for other dishes.
4. Eat at home before you go and eat lightly at the restaurant – maybe a baked potato.
5. Ask for fresh lemon wedges for your water.
6. If going to someone's house, offer to bring the salad, fill up on it then sample their offerings.
7. At a Mexican restaurant, get the salsa and guacamole side orders and eat it with the free chips!
8. Go to one of those "all-you-can-eat" Chinese places. Eat the veggies raw like a salad.
9. Bring your own dressings.
10. Explain kindly to your friends and family what you are trying to do. You may be surprised by their interest to join you.

HELPFUL KITCHEN EQUIPMENT

- Juicer. I recommend a Champion; it makes nut butters and banana ice creams.
- Dehydrator. I recommend Excalibur; they have temperature controls. Remember not to go above 110 degrees.
- Small metal mesh strainer to strain your juice.
- Large plastic storage bowls.
- Blender for smoothies and dressings.
- Food processor.
- Serrated knife.
- Garlic press.
- Canning jars for dressings, juices and nut butters.
- Parchment paper for lining dehydrator trays.
- Salad dressing carafes. You can buy these at thrift stores.
- Spiral Slicer by Joyce Chen

Chapter 7
The Testimonies

Recipes for Health

Thank God For RAW

Gloria Eden, R.N.
Hallelujah Acres
Health Care Ministry
Age 64

Gloria was inspired to get healthy when she learned that John (now her husband) was 10 years younger than she.

Gloria Eden was a spoiled kid. She'll tell you. "I got to eat anything I wanted to eat and do anything I wanted to do. If I didn't want to eat something, it was okay. When I got into school, if I didn't want to take gym class (which I didn't because I didn't like to sweat), that was okay; we got a note from the doctor. I lived my whole life indulging myself," she says.

Without a clue of what she wanted to do after high school, Gloria went into nursing school because her best friend did. She attributes her success in classes like anatomy and biochemistry to her natural curiosity about the workings of the body and to "the best high school chemistry teacher you can ever imagine."

To help her get up when she was on call and sleep when the day was dawning, Gloria used pills. "Nurses and doctors do not take care of themselves. I think there is a feeling that we know everything so nothing is going to attack us," she surmises.

Nutritionally, Gloria says she learned nothing in college. She cites vanity as her motivator for staying in shape. "It had nothing to do with my health. It all had to do with my vanity. Everything for me was exterior." Gloria says she maintained her weight through whatever means it took and tried every diet that came along.

Eventually, Gloria was diagnosed with an ulcer. She says, "People with ulcers are like the walking wounded. You look wonderful on the outside. No one would know you were sick. But it is miserable on the inside."

Thank God For RAW

When Gloria met her husband, she determined she had to be well. It didn't bother John that Gloria was 10 years his senior, but it mattered to her. She took traditional medicines for five years to combat her various ailments but grew progressively worse. She quit the home party business she had made a success because she was physically unable to continue.

In 1990, Gloria learned about nutritional health from some friends who were looking at alternatives for themselves. They shared videos, which to Gloria, made good sense. It was also at that time that Gloria read Harvey Diamond's book *Fit For Life*. "Coupled with what I knew about the body," Gloria says, "I wondered, as I devoured this information, where it had been my whole life."

"The sad thing to me, knowing what I know now, is the wasted years," Gloria acknowledges. Those years are all there for a reason and she is grateful she didn't get sicker than she did. She admits she was heading in that direction.

Gloria teaches anyone who will listen that a healthy lifestyle takes effort, a willingness to change, and ongoing education. Besides being trained as a health minister for Hallelujah Acres, her continuing education includes courses in alternative medicine, herbology, and traditional Chinese medicine.

Gloria drinks two glasses of carrot juice each day, which she considers a maintenance amount. With the carrots, she likes to include spinach and kale, celery and parsley. She takes three tablespoons of Barleygreen a day; one in the morning, one around 1 p.m., and another around 4 or 5 p.m. She enjoys all kinds of fresh fruits and vegetables and is especially fond of strong seasonings like garlic, horseradish, ginger and onion in her salad dressings. Her exercise routine includes stretching, the mini-trampoline and vigorous walking.

Gloria says, "I really feel if you have your health you can do anything. But if you don't feel well, it impacts every area of your life and not only your life but the lives of those around you—your kids, your family. It would seem to me that people who have family, and we all have family who care about us and who need us, would make every effort to be healthy.

"I always ask the Lord to bring me people who He wants me to help. Sometimes, the ones who are the most negative going in and think I'm an idiot are the strongest on the other side."

Duane Crabbs
Age 40, Pastor,
South Street Ministries
Lisa Crabbs
Age 43
Home school Mom
Children: Joshua, 15;
Bethany, 13; Hannah, 9;
Jonathan, 7

Lisa's bout with gall bladder disease and their daughter's abnormal blood tests catapulted Duane and Lisa to a new way of eating.

Duane Crabbs is a former firefighter "turned minister," who didn't eat his vegetables. He drank two pots of coffee a day and never had any significant health problems. His blood pressure was a little high and his quickened pulse rate caused concern. He took daily naps to revive himself. But, he wasn't under a doctor's care, so he thought he was doing okay and he had no intention of changing his diet.

Lisa Crabbs, on the other hand, considered herself a healthful eater. She was even a vegetarian for a while. But she ended up with a diseased gall bladder, which left her waking up tired and sick every day. When the prescription medication her doctor gave her made her very ill, his only suggestion short of surgery was that she avoid eating certain foods and wait to see if the condition corrected itself over time.

Meanwhile, their daughter, Hannah, then eight, was diagnosed with mononucleosis. Lisa says, "Hannah was always a sickly child. She'd had her tonsils removed, and suffered from ear and sinus infections. She was always on antibiotics to the point where some of them weren't working anymore." Lisa researched mono and learned that Hannah had a suppressed immune system. When a blood work-up resulted in abnormal findings, Lisa knew it was time to take immediate action.

Enter Julie Wandling.
Julie and Lisa talked about their common health issues, and Julie suggested Lisa talk with

Julie's mom, Gloria Eden. Soon Duane and Lisa were watching George Malkmus' video and reading his book, *God's Way to Ultimate Health*, and were introduced to the concept of eating primarily fresh fruits and vegetables. Lisa's first thought was, "There is no way I can take all these (cooked) foods out of my diet! What is there left to eat?" But she decided to give it a try. Duane came alongside, if only because he wasn't willing to take over the responsibility of cooking for the family. Lisa describes them as the "salami, chip chop ham, frosted flakes family" and Duane and Lisa were in agreement that their diet could stand to be "cleaned up a little."

Duane and Lisa are taking their family through the process in stages. The first thing to go was the meat, and about a month later, the dairy. Lisa says once she stopped eating dairy, she felt tremendous. They incorporated more fresh fruits and vegetables into their diet, and carrot juice and Barleygreen are now daily requirements.

Duane has substituted lots of distilled water for the coffee he used to drink. He consumes 12 to 15 glasses of water every day.

"Since I started this journey of healthful eating about a year ago, it is very seldom that my gall bladder bothers me," Lisa explains. "Hannah's health has improved immensely. The last blood test showed that she is fine." Duane's blood pressure went from the 150/100 range to 120/70 and his resting pulse rate from 74 down to 60. He attributes his increased energy to his three aerobic and weight-lifting workouts a week, his ability to keep regular sleep hours and his diet.

Duane and Lisa are quick to point out they are not over-zealous about their diet. Not all of their children have embraced this way of eating for themselves, and the parents are not demanding they do. Their goal is to keep their children with them in the process and trust they will eventually decide for themselves to eat as healthfully as they have been taught.

Each morning they prepare carrot juice, which Duane and Lisa combine with apple juice for the kids and various greens for themselves. The kids have at least two pieces of fresh fruit before eating anything else. An afternoon meal may be fresh vegetables wrapped in a tortilla shell, and dinner may include homemade pizza, whole grain pasta, stir fry or baked white or sweet potatoes. "The kids know the drill," Lisa says. "Eat your salad first."

Snacks are always available. Throughout the day the kids munch on fresh fruit, organic raisins, almonds, granola with rice milk, soy yogurt, rice or almond cheese. They leave home with these foods in their backpacks so they won't be tempted to eat something less nutritious.

While Duane and Lisa are glad to share the benefits of eating raw fruits and vegetables, their primary focus remains on being urban missionaries. They frequently have guests in their home, but food is not the topic of conversation unless they are asked to talk about it. They're careful not to come across as extreme. "We've found our own balance," Duane explains, "and our balance has shifted over time toward more raw foods. But, it's been an honest process."

Thank God For RAW

Becky Storrow
Age 36
Home school Mom
Husband: Rich
Children: Caitlin, 9;
Luke, 6; Carley, 3

When the diagnosis was multiple sclerosis, Becky became determined to allow God's healing foods to abate the symptoms of her disease.

When the first signs of Multiple Sclerosis (MS), surfaced Becky was just 23. MS is a chronic disease which damages the myelin sheath of the central nervous system. She became very ill, developed swollen tonsils and finally lost all but peripheral vision in her left eye. She underwent a series of tests, which resulted in her being sent to a specialist. Becky remembers sitting in the examining room, wondering how she was going to come up with the money to pay for these tests, which seemed to be identical to the tests she had already gone through. The doctor came in to talk with her and told her that the results confirmed a condition that was rare but sometimes found in young people called… She was alone, crying and young…she didn't catch the name of the condition that was affecting her eyesight. In retrospect, though, she's sure the two initials the doctor used were "MS." "They didn't send me to anyone else," Becky recalls, "and they said it would probably clear up in a month or two, so I went home to ride out the storm."

The next symptom was numbness in her arm. This lasted for a month or so and then subsided. But eventually half of her body became numb.

Symptoms came and went. The optic neuritis returned after the birth of Caitlin. When Luke was born, Becky was sure she had colon cancer. A constant tightness in her abdomen drew her attention to what she was eating. During this time, Becky's dad had been diagnosed with prostate cancer so during a visit she borrowed from him some of the information he had gathered in seeking his own return to health.

Thank God For RAW ▼

Among the resources were George Malkmus' video about the "Hallelujah Diet" and the book, *Fit for Life* by Harvey Diamond. Becky thought as she watched the tape, "That's it! That's what we needed to hear!"

Together, Rich and Becky committed to change the way they ate. The problem for them was the lack of support. Becky says, "A lot of people were negative, and we let that influence us." Her nightly salads got smaller and cooked portions larger. They didn't juice so often. Meat made a slight comeback in their diet.

Their third child, Carley, was born in 1998. Becky had a hard time walking as she held the baby at night. She couldn't stand well and often tripped because her lower body was numb. Then her balance went. By this time, Becky was aware of MS, knew what the symptoms were, and guessed that was what she was dealing with. But as symptoms again subsided, she put off the tests that would confirm a diagnosis for another two years.

Once Becky knew for certain she had multiple sclerosis, her doctor placed her on Avonex and steroids. During this time, Becky had learned of Hallelujah Health Seekers, a support group that advocates the lifestyle she had begun five years earlier. Carrot juice and raw fruits and vegetables have regained their place of prominence in Becky's diet. Peer pressure has become a positive element for her as she surrounds herself with people who share a common approach to health.

But for Becky a conflict arose. If raw fruits and vegetables are so healing, how do drugs fit into the equation? The test results would provide the answer to that question.

An MRI did not reveal the remission they were hoping for, and the symptoms were worsening. Becky's gait showed signs of weakening, and she was no longer able to take the dog on their morning walk around the neighborhood.

When the doctor recommended a different drug and six months of steroid infusions, Becky dared to say no. She and Rich had determined that instead of drugs, which functioned only to delay disability, she would feed her cells living food.

Becky describes her diet now as "90 percent raw." She drinks six to eight glasses of carrot juice with greens and has three to four tablespoons of Barleygreen each day. She prepares some cooked vegetarian foods for her children, who also have a daily portion of juice, Barleygreen and raw foods.

When asked how she feels today, Becky says, "Free!" Her outlook is positive and the laughter that had eluded her is back. Multiple Sclerosis is still a nemesis Becky must reckon with every day, but she's armed for battle and is confident about the future.

Becky claims Philippians 4:13 as a constant source of encouragement: "I can do all things through Christ who strengthens me."

Thank God For RAW

Diana Hamman
Age 54
Caregiver

Diana was faced with one of the biggest decisions she ever had to make when she heard the dreaded words, "breast cancer."

Diana credits progesterone cream as one of the reasons for being alive today. She was rubbing the cream into her skin when she felt the lump in her breast.

Why she got breast cancer, Diana does not know. She ate well, taught aerobics, took care of herself and didn't get sick. However, she considers herself driven and prone to anger and stress. And it ran in her family with her mom.

Years before being diagnosed with cancer, Diana worked for a chiropractor. There she learned about alternatives to traditional medicine. She remembered the advice of one of the chiropractors who said, *"Don't ever let them give you chemo. It's poison."* Even then Diana wondered if she would have the courage to stray from the conventional route if ever faced with the decision.

Confronted with the decision, she chose to have a mastectomy and reconstructive surgery. "I had gotten away from my background in alternative medicine," Diana explains, "and I never considered not having the surgery. The lump just made me crazy. I had to get rid of it!" The surgery was a success, although for a year afterward she experienced persistent discomfort in her abdomen, where fatty tissue was removed and transplanted into her breast. But, the post-operative reports were dismal. Diana was told that nine out of 13 lymph nodes contained cancer cells, and the position of the cancerous nodes indicated the cancer had spread significantly. An oncologist was immediately sent in to see Diana. "This

woman just scared me to death," Diana recalls. "She insisted that if I didn't do everything they told me, the worst would happen – like it was gospel!" As a result, Diana considered chemotherapy.

Just five days after returning home from the hospital, Diana received a phone call from a nurse she didn't know. The nurse was given Diana's name from a woman whose name was also unfamiliar to Diana. The two women spoke for an hour about their common illness, and when they were finished, Diana says there was no doubt in her mind that she would take the alternative approach to overcoming cancer. "After that conversation, I never looked back," Diana recalls.

The news to "go natural" was hard for her family to accept. But, she says, ultimately they supported her in her decision.

Diana's regimen began with a healthy diet and $400 worth of supplements each month. She was listening to the radio one day when she heard an interview with a psychologist she knew years earlier when living in Virginia. The interview wasn't about cancer, but the woman happened to mention she'd had the disease and was taking the "natural approach" to wellness. Diana called her and inquired about her program. The woman told her about George Malkmus' book *God's Way to Ultimate Health*. "This is too far out for me," Diana thought as she read the book. "I can't eat all raw food!"

Diana drinks an average of three glasses of carrot juice a day. She likes to include beets, broccoli (she juices the stalks instead of throwing them away), spinach and celery. While she eats some cooked food—chips and salsa are a weakness, she says—her diet consists primarily of fresh fruits and vegetables. She takes two tablespoons of Barleygreen daily and continues to use progesterone cream.

"If I found out today that I had cancer again," Diana says, "my changes would be to drink eight glasses of carrot juice a day instead of three and to eat no cooked food. I would never take $400 worth of supplements."

Diana sees her healing as a process God has led her through. Today, three years after being diagnosed with cancer, she is cancer-free and offers support to those who come to her with their questions about alternatives. And the process continues.

Psalm 118:17 is a verse Diana recites with gladness, "I will not die but live, and will proclaim what the Lord has done."

Thank God For RAW

Carolyn Lauer
Age 51
Home school Mom
Husband: Doug
Children: Brendan, 22;
Shannon, 20; Meghan, 16;
Caitlin, 14

Raw beets opened Carolyn's eyes to the healing capabilities of raw foods.

Carolyn Lauer woke up one morning to a month's worth of mail on the table and realized something was wrong. "I was not functioning," she recalls. Sorting through some tough issues and recovering from a difficult pregnancy took its toll on Carolyn-physically and emotionally.

God always met her needs. "I can remember praying to Him, '*I need to fix dinner and I can't even think of what to do next.*' **Go fix spaghetti** *would pop into my mind and I'd think, 'Oh, I can do that. I'll go make spaghetti.*'"

Carolyn's friend, Diana, suggested she eliminate dairy from their diet. For someone who grew up drinking milk instead of water, this was a stretch, but the results were evident. "The change was miraculous," Carolyn says. "My mind started to clear within the week."

Diana introduced Carolyn to Kathy, who owned a natural bakery. Kathy was influential in many of the nutritional improvements Carolyn made early on.

Over time she learned sugar, wheat and yeast were also affecting her family's health. The chronic ear infections, emotional outbursts, croup, cold symptoms and constipation subsided when they avoided these foods.

Carolyn had learned how to cook with vegetables, but says she wasn't yet convinced it was wise to eliminate meat from their diet. She was concerned when Meghan had developed a

love for animals that made her determined never to eat meat.

Through Julie Wandling, Carolyn was introduced to the Hallelujah Health Seekers support group. Julie's mom, a health minister with Hallelujah Acres, addressed the health issues regarding meat and educated Carolyn on the health benefits of eating raw fruits and vegetables instead. "This is good news!" Carolyn thought. "I don't have to cook anymore!"

Carolyn was open to the idea of eating raw foods for another reason. Four years earlier, she had been to a park and was stung on the leg. There developed what Carolyn could only describe as a "weird, rash-like condition," and, later, as her doctor examined it, the condition spread until it covered the entire half of her leg. Carolyn says the only thing the doctor knew to do was prescribe an antibiotic, and that was no guarantee because they had no idea what the source of the condition was.

"I was sworn off antibiotics," Carolyn states. "There had been times when Meghan was on antibiotics for a month or more, and they didn't help. Sometimes she seemed to be getting better, but I could see she was actually getting worse."

Diana suggested a remedy for Carolyn's swollen leg. Beets. Raw beets.

Carolyn knew it wouldn't kill her to eat raw beets. They weren't poisonous or anything, so she gave them a try. The rash went away. "It didn't go away all at once, but there was a very definite difference in one day and within three days it was gone," she recalls.

The incident left her amazed, saying, "*I didn't know you could eat beets raw.*" But she didn't equate that to the health-inducing benefits of a daily diet of raw fruits and vegetables until years later.

Today, Carolyn and her family have carrot juice and Barleygreen every day. They eat fruit and salads for the most part but maintain the family tradition of homemade pizza on Saturdays, just with alternative cheeses. When packing for one of their several missions trips, they're sure to include bags of dried fruit, granola and barley green tablets.

"My goal has always been to serve God," Carolyn says. "If it means eating raw fruits and vegetables to stay healthy, I'll do it. If it means eating the food that a Chinese person places in front of me, I'll do that. I won't eat dairy products, though. If I know there's milk in it, I'll say, '*I'm sorry. If I eat this dairy, I'm not going to function tomorrow. And I need to function tomorrow*'."

Carolyn says the answers came when she went to God. "When I asked Him," she says, "the information was there. It always came through other people. It didn't come through any traditional or medical means; it always came from a friend or acquaintance."

"God has always been very good about providing."

Chapter 8
The Recipes

Recipes for Health

Drinks

Carrot Juice

First thing in the morning, carrot juice is a great pick-me-up! Mix in some greens for calcium and an apple for sweetness and you're on your way to a great day! This drink is vitamin and mineral loaded. Who needs coffee?

Wait at least a half hour after drinking juice to let it assimilate into your bloodstream before eating.

Almond Milk

Raw almonds-blanched almonds by dropping into boiling water, count to 30 and remove.
Pop skins off.
Put almonds in blender with water to cover and blend until creamy.
Strain.
1 tsp vanilla (optional)

Options:
Add bananas or strawberries before blending.
Babies love this in their bottles.

Recipes for Health

Drinks

Gramps's Lemonade

1 large bunch white grapes, juiced
6 lemons, juiced
3 oranges, juiced
¼ c maple syrup
water to dilute to taste

Store in fridge. Keeps 3 days.

Water

Distilled or Reverse Osmosis

Lots of water all day. Get in the habit of carrying water bottles with you everywhere!

Recipes for Health

Seasonings

Italian:
dried basil, oregano, parsley, garlic flakes, onion flakes, ground flax and fennel seeds, in coffee grinder.

Mix all and store in a shaker bottle.

Mexican:
Cayenne powder, red pepper flakes, parsley, garlic flakes, onion flakes, ground cumin and sesame seeds, in coffee grinder.

Mix all and store in a shaker bottle.

Seaweed:
Kelp powder, dulse powder, ground sesame and/or flax seeds, in coffee grinder.

Mix all and store in a shaker bottle.

Pine Nut Parmesan:

Pine Nuts pulsed in the food processor-don't over process-they get creamy .
Sea Salt-pulse in.

Recipes for Health

Seasonings

Salad Spice

sesame seeds
paprika
poppy seeds
red pepper flakes
celery seed

Grind all in coffee grinder.

Sweet Sprinkles

sesame seeds
date sugar

Blend in coffee grinder until powdery.

Use your imagination. Sprinkle on frozen banana ice cream, apple crisp, raw pumpkin pie, etc.

Recipes for Health

Meals

Just Fruit: Any kind of fruit. As much fruit as you want.
If, at least a half-hour after you've eaten your fruit, you're still
hungry, go with one of these:

Apple Cinnamon Oatmeal

oat groats, or steel cut oats, or regular old-fashioned rolled oats
apple cider or fresh apple juice to cover oats
tad bit of honey
pinch sea salt
dried apple pieces
chopped walnuts
raisins
pinch cinnamon

Mix oats, juice, honey and salt. Let soak overnight in fridge. Add
apples, walnuts, raisins and cinnamon in the morning and enjoy at
room temperature.

Recipes for Health

Meals

Blueberries-n-Cream Oatmeal

oat groats, or steel cut oats, or regular old-fashioned rolled oats
vanilla soy or rice milk to cover
maple syrup to lightly sweeten
pinch of sea salt
dried blueberries
sliced almonds

Mix all but almonds. Let soak overnight in fridge. Top with sliced almonds in the morning and enjoy at room temperature.

Kids' Pancakes

Arrowhead Mills whole-grain pancake mix
water
options to add:
fresh or frozen blueberries
mashed banana and cinnamon, nutmeg

Pan-fry the pancakes in butter or a non-stick skillet.
Serve with pure maple syrup.

Recipes for Health

Meals

Grits and Sausage

Organic yellow corn grits cooked in water according to package directions.

BOCA sausages heated in a non-stick pan.

Cinnamon Toast

Ezekeil 4:9 sprouted bread by *Food for Life*
raw honey
cinnamon

Toast the bread. Use the honey like butter and sprinkle with cinnamon.

Recipes for Health

Meals

All Fruit Salad

1 cantaloupe
1 honeydew
1 pineapple
3 starfruit
1 pomegranate, seeds only
green grapes
red grapes
3 kiwis

Use your imagination or just what's in the fridge!
Cut everything into chunks or slices, mix and store in a huge covered storage bowl in the fridge.

Cantaloupe Bowls

Cut a cantaloupe in half.
Scoop out the seeds and discard.
Scoop out the flesh with a spoon in large chunks leaving some behind to keep the walls of the bowl stronger.
Cut flesh into small pieces and mix with other fruits.
Fill the two bowls to serve.

Recipes for Health

Meals

Pineapple Boat

Leave the top of the pineapple on.
Lay it down and slice off lengthwise just above the top.
Scoop the flesh from the small piece you removed and discard the skin.
Scoop the flesh from the big piece to make a bowl, with the top still on.
Cut the pineapple into chunks, discarding the tough core or save it for making juice.

Mix the pineapple chunks with red or purple grapes, fill the boat.
For a pretty presentation, put kale on a glass platter then top with the pineapple boat.

Tangerine Salad

6-8 tangerines peeled, sectioned, seeds removed gently
4 bananas, sliced thick, sprinkle with fresh lemon juice
1 c pineapple chunks
3 mangos, in small chunks
¼ c raisins
¼ c shredded, unsulphured, unsweetened coconut

Mix all, drizzle with honey and top with sliced almonds.

Recipes for Health

Meals

Apple Raisin Walnut Salad

Marinade:
Naysoya Nayonaise and raw honey mixed to taste.

Salad:
chopped apples
chopped celery
raisins
chopped walnuts

Mix all.

Strawberry/Tangerine Salad

baby greens
strawberries, sliced thin
tangerines, sliced thin
pine nuts
Pink Poppy dressing (page 130)

Recipes for Health

Meals

Fruit Kebabs

shiskebab skewers
chunks of cantaloupe, honeydew, pineapple, apples (sprinkled with lemon juice)
whole strawberries

Fruitify

by Kris (age 14)

2 bananas, sliced and sprinkled with lemon juice
1 apple, sliced and sprinkled with lemon juice
1 orange, sectioned and seeded
2 kiwis, peeled and sliced
5 luscious strawberries, sliced
1 c red grapes

Mix all and serve.

Recipes for Health

Meals

Marinated Rainbow Chard

1 bunch rainbow chard, chopped fine
1 red bell pepper, sliced thin
1 onion, ringed fine

Marinade:
$^1/_8$ c shoyu or tamari
$^1/_8$ c grapeseed or walnut oil
$^1/_8$ c raw honey
1 clove garlic
juice of 1 lemon

Marinate 2 hours in fridge. Great the next day.

Marinated Snow Peas

1 lb snow peas
1 onion, ringed thin
$^1/_8$ c shoyu or tamari
$^1/_8$ c olive oil
juice of ½ lemon
sesame seeds

Mix all and marinate 2 hours. Great the next day.

Recipes for Health

Meals

Shrooms

mushrooms
celery, chopped
tomatoes, chopped
onion, chopped
green pepper, chopped

Marinade:
shoyu or tamari
olive oil or sesame oil
parsley
1 clove garlic, pressed

Mix equal amounts of shoyu and olive oil. Add parsley and garlic.
Marinate 2 hours.

Recipes for Health

Meals

Marinated Turnip Greens

1 bunch turnip greens, chopped fine or large
1 onion, ringed thin
1 red bell pepper, sliced thin

Marinade:
juice of 1 lemon
1 tsp grated ginger
1 clove garlic, pressed
¼ c olive oil
2 T shoyu or tamari
1 T raw honey

Marinate 2 hours. Great the next day.

Recipes for Health

Meals

Grandma's Cucumbers

Marinade:
¼ c apple cider vinegar
2-3 T raw honey, more or less to taste
1 tsp. shoyu or tamari

Whisk together

Salad:
4 cucumbers, (peeled if not organic), sliced thin
1 large onion, sliced thin
1 T poppy seeds

Mix salad with marinade.
Marinate for 1-2 hours. Great the next day.

Recipes for Health

Meals

Stuffed Jalapenos

6 jalapenos halved lengthwise, seeds and stems removed

Stuffing:
1 avocado
juice of ½ a lemon
dash sea salt

Stuff peppers and top with ground sunflower seeds.

Eggplant Bread

1 eggplant, peeled and sliced into ½-inch thick rounds.
Marinate in shoyu or tamari for 15 minutes.
Lay slices onto dehydrator trays.
Sprinkle with sesame seeds.
Dehydrate approximately 6 hours until firm on one side, then flip and
dehydrate until chewy.

Recipes for Health

Meals

Veggie Kebabs

shiskebab skewers
slices of green, red, yellow and orange bell peppers
whole mushrooms
whole cherry tomatoes
chunks of zucchini, yellow squash
slices of onion

Marinate in dressing from Asian Pear/Spinach Salad or your favorite.

Corn Chowder or Corn Chews

2 c raw corn (off-the-cob)
1 jalapeno (optional)
dash sea salt or tamari

Run the Champion juicer with the blank screen in place. Eat as is for chowder.

For Chews: spoon out onto parchment paper-lined dehydrator trays and flatten. Dry approximately 6 hours until firm on one side then flip and continue drying until chewy/crispy.

Option: Add ground sunflower seeds before drying.

Recipes for Health

Meals

Wild Rice

wild rice
water to cover by 1 inch

Soak 4 hours then sprout until chewy.
Can add chopped vegetables, thawed frozen peas, after draining or
serve with any of the Marinated Greens recipes or Shrooms.

(Sprouting directions on page 29)

Romaine Roll-Ups

romaine lettuce leaves
mashed avocado
fresh salsa (page 115)

Spread avocado onto lettuce, top with fresh salsa, roll-up lengthwise
and serve.

Recipes for Health

Meals

Carrot Pulp Patties

3-4 c carrot pulp left from juicing, (I leave in the greens and apple pulp, too.)
½ - ¾ c sunflower seeds, ground in coffee grinder
handful flax seeds, ground in coffee grinder
shoyu or tamari
onion, chopped
celery, chopped
red bell pepper, chopped
1 clove garlic, pressed
parsley

Mix all, form into flat patties and dehydrate 4-6 hours flipping once halfway through.
Recipe adapted from *The Raw Gourmet's SunGarden Burgers*.

Recipes for Health

Meals

Salad Burritos

whole-grain burritos
romaine lettuce, shredded
green onions, chopped
black olives, sliced
raw corn (optional)
rice or soy sour cream
salsa
shredded almond, soy or rice cheddar cheese

Spread sour cream onto burrito and fill with salad and toppings.
Roll up.

Judy's Mediterranean Wraps

1 eggplant, peeled and chopped
1 tomato, chopped
2 cloves garlic, minced
juice of 1 lemon
2-4 T raw tahini
dash sea salt
4 dates, chopped
Process all in food processor with the "S" blade. Roll sauce, olives,
other chopped or shredded vegetables in lettuce leaves.

Recipes for Health

Meals

Carrot Pulp Patty/Kraut Sandwiches

carrot Pulp Patties
raw sauerkraut
sprouts
dijon mustard
dino kale leaves
caraway seeds

Spread mustard onto kale leaves, put a Carrot Pulp Patty on one end, top with kraut, sprouts, caraway seeds and roll up.

Butternut Squashta

1 Butternut Squash, peeled-cut off at the bulb, spiral slice the trunk into thin strands
Olive or walnut oil
4 cloves garlic
1 T parsley
juice of 1 lemon plus 1tsp lemon zest
Pine Nut Parmesan .
Drizzle with oil, pour in lemon juice, press garlic in and top with parsley. Sprinkle on Pine Nut Parmesan

Recipes for Health

85

Meals

Spaghetti Salad

whole grain, spelt or wheat pasta, cooked and cooled
chunks of veggies:
zucchini
yellow squash
broccoli
cucumbers, peeled if not organic
red, yellow, orange, green peppers, sliced thin
carrots, shredded
cherry tomatoes, cut in half
red onion, ringed thin
black olives, cut in half
almond, soy or rice mozzarella cheese (optional)
rice parmesan cheese (optional)

Toss with Tomato Pablano Vinaigrette (page 129)

Recipes for Health

Meals

Pesto Pasta Salad

Salad:
1 lb whole-grain pasta, cooked and cooled
½ head broccoli, chopped
1 zucchini, chopped
1 cucumber, peeled if not organic, chopped
black olives, cut in half
cherry tomatoes, cut in half
½ red bell pepper, sliced thin
1 carrot, shredded
½ a red onion, ringed thin

Pesto:
1 c fresh basil leaves
½ c fresh parsley
¼ c rice Parmesan cheese
¼ c olive oil
¼ c water
¼ c pine nuts
1 clove garlic
½ tsp sea salt
¼ tsp pepper or papaya seeds

Blend pesto in blender or processor until creamy.

Toss salad with pesto. Chill several hours, stirring often for flavors to blend.

Recipes for Health

87

Meals

Pesto Roll-Ups

large spinach leaves or dino kale
thick piece of rice, almond or soy mozzarella cheese
pesto from Pesto Pasta Salad recipe

Spread leaves with pesto, put a slice of cheese at one end and roll up. Hold with a toothpick.

Fran's Favorite Pitas

whole grain pitas
carrots, grated
shredded almond, rice or soy cheddar cheese
raisins
pine nuts
sunflower seeds
Naysoya Nayonaise
alfalfa sprouts

Mix all and stuff into whole grain pitas.

Recipes for Health

Meals

Squashta

Squashta:
1 large zucchini
1 large yellow squash

Peel both with a vegetable all the way down to the seeds into long strips or spiral slice. Top with sauce.

Sauce:
1½ c fresh tomatoes
1½ c sundried tomatoes, soaked in water for 2 hours, undrained
¾ c basil, fresh
1½ T lemon juice
1½ T olive oil
4 pitted dates

Blend sauce in blender or food processor.

Sauce can also be poured onto hot spaghetti squash.

Recipes for Health

Meals

Pizza

½ c sun-dried tomatoes, soaked in water overnight and drained
1 Tomato
3-5 Dates
½ c Walnuts
1 clove Garlic
1T Italian Herbs
Water to process
Zucchini and Yellow Squash Circles
Sliced Black Olives
Chopped Onions

Blend first 7 ingredients in food processor until rich and creamy.
Spread onto circles and top with sliced olives and chopped onions.

Corbin's Cashew Butter/Banana Sandwich

by Corbin (age 9)

2 slices whole grain bread – toasted
raw cashew butter
1 banana, sliced

Assemble sandwich.

Recipes for Health

Meals

Almond Butter/Honey Sandwich

2 slices whole grain bread
raw honey
raw almond butter

Assemble sandwich.

Ryan's Cashew Butter Jelly Sandwich

by Ryan (age 6)

2 slices whole grain bread
raw cashew butter
fruit juice-sweetened grape jelly or fresh jam

Assemble sandwich.

Recipes for Health

Meals

The Wonderful Bagel Sandwich

by Joshua (age 14) and Bethany (age 12)

1 whole grain bagel
butter
1 slice of zucchini
1 tomato
2 green onions
spinach leaves
romaine lettuce leaves
mozzarella almond cheese
Annie's Natural Ranch Dressing
garlic salt

Toast bagel and butter it. Add zucchini as a base; if you don't it will fall apart. Next add thinly sliced tomato. Finally, add chopped green onions and a few leaves of spinach and romaine. Top with the mozzarella cheese and dressing. Shake on garlic salt. Serve warm.

Recipes for Health

Meals

Corn Cabbage Relish/Salad

10 ears fresh corn, cut off the cob
1 red bell pepper, diced
1 yellow bell pepper, diced
1 green pepper, diced
1 head cabbage, finely shredded in the food processor
1 T celery seeds
1 T mustard seeds, ground in coffee grinder
½ c raw apple cider vinegar
½ c raw honey

Whisk together vinegar and honey. Pour over salad, marinate 2 hours and serve.

Mangos and Greens

any salad greens
red onion, ringed thin
mango, peeled and sliced thin
pumpkin seeds

Serve with Spicy Hoisin Dressing *(page 125)*

Recipes for Health

Meals

Romaine Salad

romaine lettuce
red bell pepper, sliced thin
handful sunflower seeds
cucumber, peeled if not organic

Serve with Tahini Dressing. (page 126)

Honey Mustard Cole Slaw

Dressing:
equal parts raw honey, Dijon mustard, flax oil

Salad:
1 head green cabbage, thin sliced or shredded
1 head purple cabbage, thin sliced or shredded
1 red onion, ringed thin
handful raw sunflower seeds

Mix all.

Recipes for Health

Meals

Chinese Salad:

1 head Nappa cabbage, if small, use 2
1 head Bok choy, if small, use 2
1 c parsley, fresh
3 green onions, chopped
1 carrot, shredded
1 red bell pepper, thin sliced

Marinade:
¼ C shoyu
¼ C maple syrup
dash cayenne
juice of 1 orange
1 tsp grated ginger (opt)
¼ C olive oil

Toss salad in marinade, don't worry if dry.
Marinate 2 hours. Great the next day, too.

Top with sunflower seeds, chopped almonds, cashews or pumpkin seeds (optional).

Greens -n- Blueberries

mesculin or baby greens
red onion, ringed thin
red bell pepper, thin sliced
blueberries
feta cheese (optional)
pumpkin seeds

Top with Kiwi Dressing *(page 130)*

Recipes for Health

Meals

August Salad

Marinade:
1 clove garlic, crushed
¼ c fresh tomato puree, use blender
1/3 c raw apple cider vinegar
2 T raw honey
½ tsp. kelp powder
1T fresh basil
1 tsp. vegetarian worcestershire sauce (no sardines)
½ tsp. Dijon mustard
¼ tsp. hot sauce or more to taste
1 c olive oil

Blend all.

Salad:
5-6 large ripe tomatoes, sliced
1 large onion, ringed thin
1 zucchini, thin sliced
1 green pepper, thin sliced

Mix salad with marinade.
Marinate 2 hours. Great the next day.

Recipes for Health

Meals

Sprout Slaw

Salad:
1-2 heads cabbage
2 c sprouts, alfalfa, clover, radish or others
1 onion, ringed thin
1T poppy seeds

Dressing:
¼ c raw honey
¼ c raw apple cider vinegar
¼ c walnut or olive oil
¼ c water

Mix dressing, pour over salad and allow to sit in fridge for 6 hours, stirring often. Prepare early in the day for dinner.

Recipes for Health

Meals

Kimchee

1 head nappa cabbage cut into 1-inch strips
2 T sea salt
2 T hot pepper paste
1 clove garlic, pressed
1 onion, ringed thin
1 T fresh grated ginger

Not fermented:
Mix all in a large bowl and cover with water. Mix well and allow to sit overnight for flavors to blend. Keep in fridge, stirring often.

Fermented:
Mix all in a large stone bowl or crock and cover with water. Cover with plastic wrap and a dish towel. Leave out at room temperature for 2 days then stir bottom to top. Leave out 2 more days then refrigerate. If it grows mold, skim it off the top. Keeps 6 weeks.

Recipes for Health

Meals

Sauerkraut

1 head green cabbage, sliced thin
1 head purple cabbage, sliced thin
4 T sea salt or wakame leaves
1 apple, sliced thick
1 onion, ringed thin
4 c water
Save the outer leaves of the cabbage.

For hot pink kraut, use 1 green and 1 purple cabbage. For white kraut, just use 2 green cabbages.

Mix the cabbage and the salt or wakame leaves in a large stone bowl or crock. Put the large cabbage leaves on top. Cover with plastic wrap and a dish towel. Leave out at room temperature for 2 days. Stir the bottom to the top. Leave out 2 more days then refrigerate. If it grows mold, skim it off the top. Remove the apple slices and large cabbage leaves. Keeps 6 weeks.

Recipes for Health

Meals

Kraut Salad

Raw sauerkraut (recipe above)
sprouts
caraway seeds
red bell pepper, chopped fine
celery, chopped fine
onion, chopped fine

Mix all together.

Sweet Broccoli Cauliflower Salad

1 head broccoli, chopped small
½ head cauliflower, chopped small
1 red bell pepper, thin sliced
handful raisins
handful sunflower seeds
1 c Nasoya nayonaise
3 T raw honey
2 T lemon juice

Recipes for Health

Meals

Sweet Cabbage Salad

Salad:
1 head green cabbage, sliced thin
1 head purple cabbage, sliced thin
1 red onion, ringed thin
2 carrots, shredded
1 apple, shredded

Dressing:
½ c grape seed, walnut or olive oil
¼ c raw honey
½ c raw apple cider vinegar
1 T poppy seeds (optional)

Mix all and marinate 2 hours. Great the next day.

Recipes for Health

Meals

Bacony Broccoli Cauliflower Salad

1 head broccoli, chopped
½ head cauliflower, chopped
2 c thawed frozen peas
1 c Nasoya Nayonaise
2 T lemon juice
2 T raw honey
½ red onion, chopped
handful sunflower seeds
shredded almond, rice or soy cheese
handful Frontier Bac'uns
½ head romaine lettuce shredded

Mix broccoli, cauliflower, peas, nayonaise, lemon juice, honey and red onion.
In a glass bowl make layers of romaine, broccoli mix, seeds, cheese, Bac'uns and repeat.

Recipes for Health

Meals

Asian Pear/Spinach Salad

Salad:
bunch baby spinach
1 red bell pepper, thin sliced
1 red onion, ringed thin
1 asian pear, peeled and thin sliced
bean sprouts
snow peas
pumpkin seeds
sesame seeds

Dressing:
¼ c olive oil
¼ c sesame oil, not toasted
¼ c water
2 T raw honey
¼ c shoyu or tamari
¼ c rice vinegar
hot sauce to taste
2 T ginger, grated

Can dress as you serve or marinate for 1 hour.

Recipes for Health

Meals

Carrot Pulp Salad

By Gloria

Salad:
large bowl of carrot pulp, from making juice
juice of 2 apples
2 stalks celery, chopped
1 onion, chopped
¾ c raisins
1 red bell pepper, diced
½ c walnuts, chopped
anything else left in your fridge at the end of the week

Dressing:
Nasoya Nayonaise
Dijon mustard
shot of maple syrup
2 cloves garlic

Recipes for Health

Meals

Pumpkin Soup

1 pie pumpkin-cut off the top and bottom, peel, scrape out the seeds
and run through the Champion Juicer with the blank screen
1 avocado
1 small onion
2 tsp cinnamon
½ tsp nutmeg
1 tsp ginger
¼ tsp allspice
1-2 c almond milk-blanch almonds, pop off the skins, put almonds in
blender with water to thin, blend until creamy
dash sea salt (optional)

Blend all in the blender adding almond milk as needed to desired
consistency.

Recipes for Health

Meals

Greek Antipasto

3 tomatoes-hunks
1 cucumber-hunks
1 zucchini-hunks
broccoli-florets
cauliflower-florets
1 bell pepper-sliced thick
1 onion-sliced thick
whole black olives

Dressing:
2T lemon juice
2T raw apple cider vinegar or more lemon juie
1T Italian dressing
1 tsp sea salt
¼ tsp pepper
½c olive oil
2-4 drops stevia liquid

Whisk dressing and marinate antipasto 2 hours.

Recipes for Health

Meals

Squashetti Salad

Zucchini-spiral sliced into thin strands
Onion-chopped
Cucumber-chopped
Olives-sliced
Tomatoes-diced
Red Bell Peppers-chopped
Italian Dressing
Salad Spice

Toss all.

Kale Slaw

1 bunch kale, chopped fine
1 onion, chopped fine
1 red bell pepper, chopped fine
1 c sweet potato, shredded

Marinade:
juice of 1 lemon
2 T shoyu or tamari
¼ c olive oil
hot pepper sauce to taste
1 clove garlic, pressed

Marinate 2 hours. Great the next day.

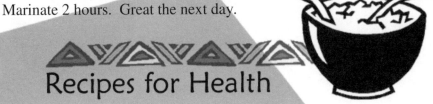

Recipes for Health

Meals

Basic Salad Greens

Organic is best, but not always available. When you can't buy organic, just be sure to wash your produce very well in ¼ c vinegar and a sinkful of water.

My favorite greens for salad:
mesculin greens
baby greens
spring mix
red leaf lettuce
green leaf lettuce
romaine lettuce
red romaine lettuce
bibb lettuce
radicchio
spinach
green cabbage
red cabbage
nappa cabbage
bok choy
endive-bitter
escarole
swiss chard
rainbow chard
butter lettuce

Recipes for Health

Snacks

Nutty Granola

4-5 c oats
¾ c buckwheat groats, soaked ½ an hour in water and rinsed well
½ c unhulled sesame seeds
¾ c raw sunflower seeds
½ c coarse, chopped raw almonds
½ c walnuts, broken up
½ c pecans, broken up
½ c ground flax seeds, ground in coffee grinder

Mix above in a large bowl.

1/3 c raw honey
2 tsp vanilla
1/3 c apple juice

Mix above then pour over granola and mix to coat.

Dry in dehydrator til crispy.

Options to add:
oat-floured date pieces
raisins
coconut

Recipes for Health

Snacks

Carob Granola

4-5 c oats
¾ c buckwheat groats, soaked ½ an hour in water and rinsed well
½ c shredded, unsulphured, unsweetened coconut
1 c coarse, chopped almonds
½ c ground flax seeds, ground in coffee grinder

Mix above in large bowl
2 T carob powder
¼ c - ½ c maple syrup

Mix above then pour over granola and mix to coat.
Dry in dehydrator til crispy.

Snappy Nuts

raw almonds or cashews
hot sauce of your choice

Soak nuts in hot sauce for 1 hour, stirring often. (Can dilute hot sauce with water for a milder flavor.) Lay out on parchment paper-lined dehydrator trays. Dry until crispy.

Recipes for Health

Snacks

Oriental Nuts

raw almonds or cashews
shoyu or tamari

Soak nuts in shoyu or tamari for 1 hour, stirring often. (Can dilute in a little distilled water for a milder flavor.) Lay out on parchment paper-lined dehydrator trays. Dry until crispy.

Judy's Almond Filled Dates

by Judy

whole pitted dates
raw almonds

Stuff each date with 1 almond.

Recipes for Health

Snacks

Ryan's Flax Figs

by Ryan (age 6)

black mission figs
ground flax seeds, (use a coffee grinder, Mom)

Roll figs in flax seeds as you eat them.

Chili Crackers

2 c almonds-ground fine
1 onion
3 roma tomatoes
3 tsp flax seeds-ground in coffee grinder
1 tsp sea salt
2 tsp chili powder

Blend all until gooey. Put out onto a teflex sheet on a dehydrator tray. Put parchment paper on top and roll thin with a rolling pin. Score into squares with a pizza cutter (now a cracker scorer). Dehydrate until crispy. Flip and dry the other side a few hours until crispy through.

Recipes for Health

Dips & Spreads

Sweet Sunflower Paté

1 c sunflower seeds
5 dates
¼ red bell pepper
1 green onion
water to thin

Blend all in the food processor until creamy. Serve stuffed into celery or spread onto red leaf lettuce leaves, rolled up. Serve to babies with a spoon.

Pimento Spread

½ head cauliflower
1 c sunflower seeds
1 red bell pepper
2 T shoyu or tamari

Blend all in blender or food processor until creamy. Serve stuffed into celery or smear onto lettuce leaves and roll up. Serve to babies with a spoon.

Recipes for Health

Dips & Spreads

Mom's Hummus

By Gloria

4 c sprouted garbanzo beans or cooked dried beans
½ c tahini
juice of 1 lemon
shoyu or tamari to taste
garlic cloves
Nasoya Nayonaise to make creamy
dash cayenne pepper

Blend all to taste in food processor until creamy. ONLY use sprouted beans if you have a heavy-duty processor. Great veggie dip. Mom even dips raw green beans.

Recipes for Health

Dips & Spreads

Fresh Salsa

3 large tomatoes, chopped fine
2 green onions, chopped fine
½ each red, yellow, orange bell peppers, chopped fine
handful cilantro
1T cumin
sea salt to taste
juice of 1 lime
1 tsp raw honey

Mix all and marinate 2-4 hours.

Raw Almond Butter

Run raw almonds through a Champion or GreenLife Juicer with the
blank screen in place. Drizzle with almond, walnut, Udo's Choice or
flax oil. Add sea salt (optional).

Cashews also make a nice nut butter.

Recipes for Health

Dips & Spreads

Fresh Jams
4 c berries
2 T agar agar
1 c apple juice

Boil juice and agar agar for 2 minutes.
Pour over fresh mashed berries and stir.
Refrigerate until set.

Apples and Almond Fluff

1 8-oz rice or tofu cream cheese, softened
¼ c raw almond butter
¼ c raw honey
dash cinnamon

Whip until fluffy in processor.
Dip with apple wedges.

Recipes for Health

Dips & Spreads

Apple Papaya Sauce

3 apples
1 papaya, flesh only, save seeds to dry
2 bananas
shot of maple syrup
dash of cinnamon
Maple Granola (optional)

Blend in blender or processor until creamy. Top with granola.

Caramel Apple Dip

½ c dates
½ c raisins
¼ c water

Blend in food processor until thick and creamy. Dip apples.

Recipes for Health

Dips & Spreads

Avocado Dip or Dressing

1 avocado
½ red bell pepper
¼ red onion
½ tsp cumin seeds or ground cumin
pinch cayenne (or more to taste)
¼ tsp sea salt
juice of ½ lemon
water to thin if for dressing

Blend in blender or processor until creamy.

Avocado Jalapeno Dip

2 avocados
1 jalapeno, no stems or seeds
juice of 1 lemon
¼ tsp sea salt

Blend in blender or processor until creamy.

Recipes for Health

Dips & Spreads

Guacamole

4 avocados, whipped in blender with juice of 1 lemon
½ tsp sea salt
1 clove garlic
1 tomato, chopped fine
½ red bell pepper, chopped fine
1 jalapeno, chopped fine

Recipes for Health

Dips & Spreads

Fruit Salsa

Inspired by the Chef Vicki at Kent State University
1 mango-peeled and diced
1 cucumber-diced
½ serrano chile, seeded and minced
½ jalapeno, seeded and minced
1/3c fresh corn
2 scallions-diced
1 clove garlic-pressed
½ red bell pepper-diced
1T fresh basil-chopped
1T fresh cilantro-choped
½c water
½c fresh mango juice
2T orange juice
2T raw apple cider vinegar
1T lemon juice
1T lime juice
1 tsp sea salt
2 drops stevia liquid (optional)

Mix all and chill ½ hour. Eat as a soup or pour over salad greens.

Recipes for Health

Dressings

DRESSING BASICS

Fats: olive oil, walnut oil, grapeseed oil, Udo's oil, avocado, almonds, sunflower seeds, cashews, pine nuts, walnuts, almond butter, tahini, cashew butter, pumpkin seeds, ground flax seeds soaked in water

Acids: lemon juice, orange juice, kiwi, strawberries, tomatoes, sun-dried tomatoes, pineapple, pineapple juice, nectarines, raw apple cider vinegar.

Sweeteners: maple syrup, raw honey, stevia, dates, raisins, prune juice, red bell pepper, mango, papaya, banana, nectarine, grapes.

Spices: garlic, onion, basil, oregano, cumin, ginger, cayenne, parsley, fennel seeds, poppy seeds, sea salt, shoyu, paprika, clery seed, dried celery, horseradish, mustard seds, red pepper flakes.

Choose one from each of the categories above and blend to your liking, tasting often.

Thinners: water, cucumber, celery, celery juice, red bell pepper juice, carrot juice, apple juice, any other juice you like.

Thickeners: boiled arrowroot powder or agar-agar, ground flax seeds, soaked sunflower seeds, soaked almonds, pumpkin seeds, walnuts, cashews, tahini, almond butter, banana, avocado.

Recipes for Health

121

Dressings

All dressings should be allowed to sit for several hours in order for the flavors to blend. I usually make them in the morning for my dinner salad.

Almond Butter Dressing

¾ c raw almond butter
4 T onion, chopped fine
2 cloves garlic
juice of 1 lemon
1 T ginger
1 T shoyu or tamari
1 T sesame oil, not roasted
1 tsp cayenne
½ c water
1 T maple syrup or 2 dates

Recipes for Health

Dressings

French Dressing

2/3 c organic fruit-sweetened catsup
½ c raw apple cider vinegar
¾ c raw honey
¼ c flax oil
1 small onion
2 tsp paprika
2 tsp vegetarian worcestershire sauce (no sardines)
¼ c water or more to thin

Mix all in blender or processor until creamy. (Ryan loves this as a dressing for carrots and broccoli mixed.)

Italian Dressing

¼c olive oil
1T honey or maple syrup
1T Italian Herbs
1 clove garlic
½ tsp dried onion or 1T diced onion
1 lemon juiced
½ tsp sea salt (opt)
1 tsp arrowroot powder boiled in ¼ c water-slightly cooled

Mix all.

Recipes for Health

Dressings

Kiwi Dressing

2 kiwis, peeled
3 T light olive oil or walnut oil
2 T raw apple cider vinegar
2 T raw honey
¼ tsp sea salt
¼ tsp pepper or papaya seeds

Blend all in blender or processor until creamy. Beautiful served over baby greens and blueberries.

Orange Mexican Dressing

½c olive oil
½c water
¼c orange juice
1T dried onion
1 clove garlic
2 tsp honey
1 tsp cumin
1 ½ tsp sea salt
1 tsp oregano
¼ tsp red pepper flakes

Mix all and chill 1 hour.

Recipes for Health

Dressings

Walnut Dressing

2 T vinegar
1 tsp lemon juice
2 tsp mustard
¼ tsp sea salt
¼ tsp pepper
1/3 c walnut oil
1 pinch tarragon

Spicy Hoisin Dressing

¼ c hoisin sauce
¼ c olive oil
¼ c rice vinegar
¼ c water
1 T fresh grated ginger
1 T orange zest
1 T diced chili pepper, pepper flakes or hot sauce
1 T pepper

Blend all in blender or processor until creamy.

Recipes for Health

Dressings

Honey Sage Dressing

1/3 c olive oil
4 cloves garlic
3 T raw apple cider vinegar
1 T lemon juice
2 tsp raw honey
1½ T fresh sage, minced
dash sea salt
pepper or papaya seeds

Blend all in blender or processor until creamy.

Tahini Dressing

¼ c lemon juice
2/3 c flax oil
2/3 c water
3 T shoyu or tamari
½ c raw tahini (sesame seed butter)
$^1/_8$ of an onion
2 cloves garlic
2 T maple syrup

Blend all in blender or processor until creamy. Can be thinned with more water if necessary.

Recipes for Health

126

Dressings

Chinese Dressing:

1/6 c sesame oil, not toasted
1/6 c olive oil
1/3 c rice vinegar
½ c shoyu or tamari
¼ c raw honey
2 T fresh grated ginger

Blend all in blender or processor until creamy.

Sweet-n-Sour Poppy Seed Dressing

2/3 c raw honey
½ tsp Dijon mustard
½ tsp sea salt
1/6 c raw apple cider vinegar
½ an onion
½ c olive or walnut oil
1 T poppy seeds

Blend all in blender or processor until creamy.

Recipes for Health

Dressings

Ginger Dressing

3 T grated ginger
½ onion
¾ c olive oil
¼ c rice vinegar
½ c shoyu or tamari
2 pieces sun-dried tomatoes, soaked in water 1 hour and drained
$^1/_8$ c lemon juice
1 clove garlic
½ c water
1 tsp hot pepper flakes or hot pepper sauce (optional)

Blend all in blender or processor until creamy.

Nectarine Dressing

2-4 Ripe Nectarines
½ lemon juiced
½ an onion
½ yellow bell pepper

Blend all in food processor until creamy.

Recipes for Health

Dressings

Tomato Pablano Vinaigrette

1/3 c raw apple cider vinegar
3 sun-dried tomatoes, soaked in water 1 hour and drained
juice of 1 lemon or 1 lime
1 ¾ tsp hot sauce
1 tsp dried onion
1 clove garlic, pressed
½ tsp sea salt
¾ c olive oil
¾ c water
1 tomato, diced
1 pablano chili, diced
1 tsp Italian seasoning or oregano

Blend all in blender until creamy.

Honey Mustard Dressing for One

1 T Dijon mustard
1 T raw honey
1 T walnut or olive oil
1 T hot water
hot sauce or cayenne (optional)

Whisk with a fork.

The kids like this as a dip for soy "chicken" nuggets or put the nuggets on their salad with this dressing.

Recipes for Health

129

Dressings

Pink Poppy Dressing

2 T raw honey
¼ c walnut or grape seed oil
juice of 1 lemon
1 T poppy seeds
¼ c water
¼ red onion
1 clove red garlic
5 strawberries, stems removed

Blend all in blender or processor until creamy.

Recipes for Health

Dressings

Grandma's Goofy Banana Salad Dressing

1 banana
¼ c raw tahini
juice of 2 lemons
2 cloves garlic
1 T shoyu or tamari
1 c water

Blend all in blender or processor until creamy.

Corbin's Creamy Dressing

by Corbin (age 9)

3 T Nasoya Nayonaise
¼ c olive oil
2 T lemon juice
1 clove garlic, pressed
dash sea salt
1 T fresh or 1 tsp dried parsley
1 T fresh or 1 tsp dried dill

Blend all in blender or processor until creamy. Makes nice veggie dip, too.

Recipes for Health

Dressings

Garlicky Cuke Dressing

1 cucumber (peeled if not organic)
2 green onions
5 dates
juice of 1 lemon
1 T fresh or 1 tsp dried dill
1 clove garlic
water to thin

Blend all in blender or processor until creamy.

Carrot Salad with Almond Butter Dressing

4 c shredded carrots
4 green onions, diced
1 tomato, chopped
1 c thawed frozen peas
1 red bell pepper, diced

Dress with Almond Butter Dressing and serve. *(page 122)*

Recipes for Health

Sweets

Lemon Pudding

2 avocados
1 ½ c lemon flesh-no seeds
juice of 1 lemon
2 c dates
4 T maple syrup

Blend all in blender or processor until creamy.

Carob Pudding

2 avocados
¾ c maple syrup
2 T carob powder

Blend all in blender or processor until creamy.

Recipes for Health

Sweets

Smoothies

Freeze bananas in the skin or peel first and put in freezer bags. If you are lazy like me and freeze them in their skins, just run them under hot water and the skins will pop off when you need them.

Blend the following ingredients in a blender to make some terrific treats:

Carob: frozen bananas, carob powder and vanilla rice or soy milk.
Vanilla: frozen bananas, vanilla soy or rice milk.
Orange: peeled/seeded oranges, ice cubes, frozen banana.
(Sometimes we add coconut milk or dried coconut.)
Berry: frozen bananas, frozen berries (strawberry, raspberry, blueberry, blackberry: I pick and freeze tons of them when in season), vanilla soy or rice milk.
Tropical: frozen bananas, fresh or frozen mangos, pineapple, vanilla rice, soy milk or coconut milk.

Recipes for Health

Sweets

Grandma's Pecan Balls

3 bananas, mashed
2 c dates
1 c unsulphured, unsweetened shredded coconut
½ c chopped raw pecans
1 tsp vanilla
½ tsp sea salt (optional)
1 tsp cinnamon
2 c rolled oats

Mix all. Roll into balls. Refrigerate.

Apple Crisp

6 apples
1 c raisins
¼ c water
1 tsp cinnamon
2 T ground flax seeds
Blend in food processor until like applesauce.
Topping:
1c almonds
½ c dates

Blend in food processor until crumbly and sprinkle on top.

Recipes for Health

135

Sweets

Carob Cake Cookies

4 c sunflower seeds
2 c cashews
½-¾ c carob powder
2 T maple syrup or honey
2 bananas
dash sea salt (opt)
10 drops stevia (opt)
1 c dates
1 c raisins
2 tsp vanilla

Blend all in food processor until thick batter.
Drop by the teaspoonful onto dehydrator sheets.
Dehydrate 12-15 hours until cake-like.

Recipes for Health

Sweets

Apple-Cinnamon Oatmeal Cookies

1 c dates
1 c raisins
2 apples
1 tsp vanilla
1 tsp cinnamon
dash sea salt (optional)
2-3 c oats

Blend in food processor all except oats until thick batter. Stir in oats.
Form cookies with two wet teaspoons and drop onto dehydrator
sheets. Dry until desired consistency. Great to start in the early
evening and eat before bed! Then take out the rest in the morning.

Yum Yum Plum Pudding

by Corbin age 10
5 bananas
5 dates
5 plums

Blend in the blender or food processor until creamy.

Recipes for Health

Sweets

Fruit Molds

Fruit, any kind
Fresh jam, any kind (use when not quite set) *(page 116)*
Mix all and pour into a mold. Chill until set.

Orange Ice

frozen oranges, peel and seed before freezing
Run through the Champion or GreenLife juicer with the blank screen in place.

Can also make Pineapple Ice, Lemon Ice, Strawberry Ice, Cantaloupe Ice, Watermelon Ice.

Tumasickles

by Bill Tuma age 76

Carrot juice

Freeze in popsicle molds!

Recipes for Health

Sweets

Fudgesickles

4 frozen bananas
2 T carob powder
4 tsp maple syrup

Blend all until creamy. Pour into molds and freeze.

Banana Ice Cream

frozen bananas

Run through a Champion or GreenLife Juicer with the blank screen in place.

For variety you can run the following frozen fruits through the juicer with the bananas:
strawberries
kiwis
blueberries
raspberries
mangos

Or stir in carob powder and/or mint extract and/or chopped nuts.

Recipes for Health

139

Sweets

Frozen Strawberry/Banana Pie

Crust:
2 c ground almonds OR 1c ground almonds + 1 c ground sunflower seeds
1 tangerine OR orange, peeled and seeded
1 c dates
½ tsp vanilla
1 tsp cinnamon
½ c unsulphured, unsweetened, shredded coconut

Blend dates, tangerine and vanilla until creamy in blender or processor. Mix in remainder of ingredients with a fork. Press into a pie plate and freeze while making filling.

Filling:
5 frozen bananas
2 c frozen strawberries, remove tops before freezing
2 frozen kiwis, peel before freezing

Run frozen fruit through a Champion or GreenLife Juicer with the blank screen in place. Mix with a spoon. Fill the crust and refreeze for at least 1 hour.

Recipes for Health

Sweets

Ryan's 7th Birthday Cake

1 Cannonball Watermelon
Poke holes in it with a sharp thin knife.
Insert Candles.
Light up like a cannonball!

Ben's Birthday Cake
By Judy DeShon

2 cartons vanilla Soy Delicious Ice Cream, softened
1 box Midel Chocolate Crisps
½ c dates
½ c raisins
½ c pecans (optional)
1 tsp vanilla
Experiment with a ripe banana, coconut or oatmeal!

Blend chocolate crisps, dates, raisins, pecans in processor. Add vanilla.
Line the bottom of a cake pan with half the cookie mixture, top with Soy Delicious and rest of cookie mixture. Refreeze for 2 hours.

Sit out for 10 minutes before trying to slice.

Recipes for Health

141

Sweets

Carob Fudge

2 c raw almonds or cashews, soaked in water overnight
1 c dates
1 c raisins
2 T carob powder
1 c fresh pineapple juice (save those cores, can even freeze them for
this or pineapple ice)

Blend in processor, then add:
1 c flax seeds, ground in a coffee grinder

Spread on cookie sheet and freeze. When solid, cut into squares.
Store in freezer.

Recipes for Health

Sweets

Prune Chews

1 c prunes
1 c dried apples
1 c Brazil nuts or others
2 T fresh lemon juice
dash cinnamon
dash nutmeg
dash sea salt

Whiz all in processor. Make into patties and place on parchment paper lined dehydrator trays. Dry approximately 6 hours until firm on one side then flip and continue drying til crispy.

Fig Chews

½ c figs without stems
2 c unsulphured, unsweetened, shredded coconut
1 c fresh orange juice
dash cinnamon
dash sea salt

Blend all in processor. Make patties and place on parchment paper-lined dehydrator trays. Dry approximately 6 hours until firm on one side then flip and continue drying until crispy.

Recipes for Health

Sweets

Banana Cream Pie

Crust:
1 c almonds, chopped fine
1 c banana chips, chopped fine
1 c dates
dash sea salt

Blend all in processor and pat into ungreased pie plate.

Filling:
3 T arrowroot powder
1 ½ c soy or rice milk, vanilla
1 ½ T raw honey
2 tsp vanilla

Whisk until creamy and boil for 3 minutes.

Slice 3 bananas and sprinkle with fresh lemon juice. Put half the
banana slices in the bottom of the crust. Pour in the cream
filling. Top with the rest of the banana slices.

Top with shredded, unsulphured, unsweetened coconut.

Chill 4 hours and serve.

Recipes for Health

Sweets

Blueberry/Orange Cups

1 c blueberries
3 oranges
vanilla soy or rice yogurt (optional)
Maple Granola (optional)

Slice oranges in half. Carefully scoop out the flesh leaving the skin halves intact. Dice the flesh and remove the seeds. Mix orange pieces with blueberries. Fill orange skins with fruit mix. Top with yogurt and granola (optional).

Sweet Potato Crunchies

1 Sweet Potato-peeled and spiral sliced into thin strands
Toss with Sweet Sprinkles.
Dehydrate until crispy.

Recipes for Health

145

Sweets

Fresh Fruit Pie

Crust from Frozen Strawberry/Banana Pie (found on page ?).
Press crust into pie plate.

Fill with any of the following by itself or mixed with others:

grapes, red and/or green
strawberries
banana slices
kiwi slices
orange sections, seeded
pear slices
peach slices
blueberries
blackberries
raspberries

Pile the fruit HIGH

Glaze:
1 c apple juice
¼ c raw honey
1 tsp vanilla
2 T agar agar

Bring glaze to a boil for 2 minutes. Cool for 5 minutes stirring often. Pour over fruit. Put in fridge to set for at least 2 hours.

Recipes for Health

Sweets

Strawberry Pie

Crust from Frozen Strawberry/Banana Pie (found on page ?)
Press crust into pie plate
4 c strawberry slices or whole berries, or more, to fill crust

Glaze:
1 c apple juice
½ c strawberry puree, use blender or processor
¼ c raw honey
2 T agar agar

Bring glaze to a boil for 2 minutes. Cool for 5 minutes stirring
often. Pour over strawberries. Put in fridge to set for at least 2 hours.

This pie can be made with any kind of fresh berries.

Recipes for Health

Sweets

Fancy Frozen Carob/Banana Cake

12 Frozen Bananas
½ c Carob Powder
¼ c Maple Syrup

Run bananas through Champion Juicer with Blank Screen.
Stir in carob and maple syrup.

Crust and Crumbles:
3 c Almonds
1 c Dates
½ c Dried Coconut
Dash Sea Salt (optional)

Blend all in food processor until crumbly.
Press crust into a Springform Pan.
Fill ¾ of the way with Carob Banana Mixture.
Lay on a layer of crust crumbles-finish it off.

Top Layer:
4-6 Frozen Bananas
½ c Dried Coconut
Run bananas through Champion Juicer with Blank Screen. Stir in Coconut.
Put on top of crumbles and carefully spread evenly.
Sprinkle with additional coconut.
Freeze until solid.
Remove collar and slice.

Recipes for Health

Chapter

About The
Author

9

Recipes for Health

Julie Wandling, homeschool mom, age 36

At over 300 pounds, Julie used to consider herself a big girl. Then she developed toxemia and for the first time began to see herself as a sick, fat person. Now 100 pounds lighter, she identifies again with her tall, fit 17-year-old self, and she's not finished yet!

Julie's photo albums hold memories of her as a high-school majorette, smiling as she holds a rifle she twirled in parades. Ten years later, she weighed over 260 pounds. Eventually, she reached 315 pounds and had difficulty making it to the top of the stairs.

What takes a person from fit to fat? "It was just life," Julie says. When she marched in parades, she would get to the end of a route and eat four or five hot dogs and bags of potato chips and drink pop. She was hungry and that's what there was to eat. While she appeared to be fit, her cells were gradually storing the excess fat she was consuming on a regular basis.

Later, as her active life became more sedentary, her eating habits remained the same. "I started doing the cooking and baking thing," Julie says. She baked breads and cheesecakes and sold them. A favorite was her pepperoni bread with mozzarella cheese. "I'd bring 90 loaves to a flea market and sell 'em, boom, like that," she says with a laugh that's uniquely Julie. Of course, there was leftover bread and the occasional fallen cheesecake. And nothing was wasted.

Her pregnancy with her younger son, Ryan, was difficult, and after he was born, Julie developed toxemia. She was hospitalized with blood pressure that had skyrocketed past 200/100.

"At my mother's prompting," Julie recalls, "I tried a vegetarian diet." She went to the library and checked out book after book on the subject. "It was a hard diet," Julie says. "I was always having to soak beans and cook beans and make beans taste like something, and I was still using a lot of sugar and dairy products because these ingredients were called for in most of the vegetarian cookbooks."

She did lose 60 pounds on this diet, but eventually she reached a plateau and her diet

still consisted of foods that lacked nutrition.

At the same time that she was trying to figure out how she should be eating, she built a reputation on feeding others. Her catering business was thriving. She referred to herself as the "cream cheese queen" and was constantly giving recipes to those who inquired about the delicious fare she served. "I would buy this real pretty kale and I'd put it all around the trays and cover it with these cream cheese-laden things that I slaved over for hours and days. And everybody would come by and eat the nasty stuff and we'd throw away the green stuff on the bottom."

She gained back the 60 pounds she'd lost as she gave up the beans and opted instead for the food she had already prepared. There wasn't time for both. She says for two years she ate leftover party food.

The turning point for Julie came one winter day when she went to see her doctor for her annual exam. That day her blood pressure was 199/100 and her doctor instructed her to go straight to the hospital where she was to be put on blood pressure medication. She left the office with the prescription, but she didn't go to the hospital. She knew she didn't want to be on medication for the rest of her life (her dad had died at 61 from a heart attack, having been on blood pressure medication himself). Besides, the kids were with a sitter and she needed to get home.

In front of the mirror, Julie says she took a good look at herself and admitted that it was she who got herself into this mess. And she was determined to get herself out.

Julie went back to her books. At the library she looked for books that would show her how to "make things," and Julie says she realized that her mistake all along was in trying to "re-create the wheel." She explains, "God had already made me all this sweet, perfect, wonderful food. I would not just sit down and eat strawberries. I had to make a strawberry pie. I was that kind of person. It was my reputation, my way of thinking. I had to create something with it."

Julie credits her mom with introducing her to George Malkmus' "Hallelujah Diet." Malkmus and other advocates of an all-raw diet have helped her gradually regain health through a diet that consists primarily of fresh fruits and vegetables. Her transformation is the result of tireless research and a commitment to applying to her life all she learns. She has developed a ministry to help others achieve similar results through workshops and lectures. She has a passion for reaching those who are overweight as well as homeschool parents whom she advises to "train up their children in the ways of healthful eating."

Julie still enjoys feeding people. "It just makes me happy; it's a quirk of mine," she says. "But now I can create a platter with food just as God made it and it looks beautiful. All I did was cut it and arrange it, whereas God did all the work, and he gets the glory for the food, not me." "When people ask me for my old recipes now," she says, "I tell them I threw them all away. I'd rather tell them to eat some watermelon."

"This is the way God created our bodies to eat," Julie states. "I think about my own little corner of the world and the people who are in it. I know I'm going to run up against opposition, but I just want to be a testimony that this is a God-honoring way of eating. No matter how many people argue theology with me, God just didn't put Oreos and ice cream on the planet. We did. You can't argue the fact that God made watermelon grow out of the ground. He did not make cheesecake grow out of the ground. So much of what we eat comes out of a laboratory."

For Julie, there's no looking back. This isn't a diet to lose weight. She says the nutrition takes care of the cravings and desires. In the beginning, there were times when she was tempted to eat foods that would have been counterproductive to reaching her goals, but she was seeing results so quickly that mentally she didn't want the food. Now, she says, she's experienced a physiological change that has allowed her taste buds to appreciate the sweetness of prunes, figs, dates and raw almonds.

"People ask me all the time if I cheat," Julie says. "There's nothing out there that's better than what I'm eating now. For me, cheating would be eating this whole bowl of strawberries…which I probably will do."

And she laughs that laugh that is so uniquely Julie.

Thank God For **RAW** ▼

Julie's Favorite RAW Resources

Books, videos and website by Hallelujah Acres, www.hacres.com <http://www.hacres.com>
Books and videos by Dr. Doug Graham, www.doctorgraham.cc/ <http://www.doctorgraham.cc/>
Audio tapes by Dr. Joel Robbins
Diet for a New America book and video by John Robbins
The Food Revolution by John Robbins
Fit for Life I, II and A New Beginning by Harvey Diamond
The Raw Gourmet by Nomi Shannon, www.rawgourmet.com <http://www.rawgourmet.com>
Living in the Raw, Rose Lee Calabro
Living Nutrition Magazine, www.livingnutrition.com <http://www.livingnutrition.com>
All videos by Dr. Lorraine Day
Books by Norman Walker
Juiceman's Power of Juicing, Jay Kordich
www.vegsource.com <http://www.vegsource.com>
www.rawfoodsnews.com <http://www.rawfoodsnews.com>
www.madcowboy.com <http://www.madcowboy.com>
www.earthsave.com <http://www.earthsave.com>

Contact Information:

Healthy for Him
Julie Wandling & Gloria Edert
Healthy4Him@neo.rr.com
www.Healthy4Him.com

Index

Thank God For RAW

Thank God For RAW ▼